KOMODO

DATE			

Previous Books

Dick Lutz (Richard L. Lutz, MSW) is the author of *Feel Better! Live Longer! Relax*. Salem, Oregon: DIMI PRESS, 1988.

Dick and Mary Lutz are the authors of *The Running Indians*. Salem, Oregon: DIMI PRESS, 1989.

DICK LUTZ & J. MARIE LUTZ

KOMODO

THE LIVING DRAGON

DIMI PRESS
3820 Oak Hollow Lane, SE
Salem, Oregon 97302
© 1991 by Dick Lutz and J. Marie Lutz
Printed in the United States of America
First Edition, Second printing

Library of Congress Cataloging in Publication Data:

        Lutz, Richard L., 1929-
        Lutz, J. Marie, 1958-
        Komodo, the living dragon/by Dick Lutz and J. Ma-
        rie Lutz.
            p.   cm.
        Includes bibliographical references and index.
        ISBN: 0-931625-21-1 : $10.95
        1. Komodo dragon. 2. Wildlife conservation—Indo-
        nesia—Komodo Island I. Lutz, J. Marie (Judy Marie),
        1958- . II. Title.
        QL666.L29L87 1991
        333.95'7—dc20   91-6354

Cover photo by Boyd Norton
Uncredited photos by Mary Lutz
Cover design by Bruce DeRoos
Typeface 11 pt. Palatino
Printing by Patterson Printing, Benton Harbor, Michigan

DEDICATION

To **Jim, Anita, Sherry,** and **David**, who have always shared our fascination with reptiles,

and to **Mary** and **Michael**, whose loving support made this book possible.

CONTENTS

ILLUSTRATIONS

PHOTOS

MAPS

PREFACE

A number of years ago, three small children clustered around a cage filled with lizards they had believed to be mythical. Of course the baby had to be boosted up to see, but what else is a big brother for? Meanwhile the solemn-faced four-year-old and her father, tall and bespectacled, took their first look at the common green iguana. After a nine-month stay in the Sierra Madre mountains of central Mexico, they had begun to wonder if the country's most well-known lizard really existed. It took a visit to the pet shop in their new California home to confirm the story's reality. This first glimpse of exotic lizards sowed the seeds for *Komodo, The Living Dragon*.

This book is the product — for both of us — of years of fascination with reptiles and exploration. For J. Marie, the trip to the pet shop was the beginning of 23 years of raising iguanas. Our interest in Komodo dragons sprang from another shared moment, when Dick took all the children, now numbering five, south to Disneyland and then to the San Diego Zoo to see the giant Galapagos tortoise and the huge, greyish Komodo dragons.

Years later, Dick and his wife Mary visited Mexico and explored the craggy wilds of the Barrancas del Cobre. More interested in the people than in the wildlife, they wrote the book *The Running Indians, The Tarahumara of Mexico*. Their next exploration of the tropics would include a visit to Komodo Island in distant Indonesia, where they encountered Komodo dragons face to face and Dick began work on this book. The difference between Komodo dragons in the wild and in captivity was vividly illustrated when they observed the two dragons in the National Zoo in Washington, D.C., on their return to the United States. J. Marie visited the Cincinnati Zoo for additional study and direct observation of the giant monitors that inspired *Komodo, The Living Dragon*.

Both of these books -- accounts of little known living beings that have been described as primitive and ancient -- have a hopeful feeling. In the Tarahumara book, Dick and Mary focused on their belief that the Indian tribe will, in its essential characteristics, continue to survive. Likewise, this book is optimistic about the future of the great reptile described, primarily because of the enlightened policies of the nation of Indonesia. Information on ordering both books can be found in the back of this book or at any book store.

Dick Lutz - Salem, Oregon
J. Marie Lutz - Champaign, Illinois

ACKNOWLEDGMENTS

Many people helped to make this book possible. Some of them are listed below:

Dr. Dale Marcellini, Curator of the Reptile House at the National Zoo in Washington, D.C., provided valuable comments on an early draft of the manuscript. **Bela Demeter,** Keeper in the Reptile House, granted permission to use his account of the zoo bringing two Komodo dragons to the United States, which was published in *Zoogoer*, the magazine of the Friends of the National Zoo. **Kay Kenyon,** librarian at the same zoo, also assisted in our work.

Several people at the Cincinnati Zoo and Botanical Garden were extremely helpful, particularly during J. Marie's research at the zoo. These people include **Dr. Edward J. Maruska,** Executive Director; **Johnny Arnett,** Area Supervisor of Reptiles, Amphibians and Fish, and Lead Reptile Keeper **Michael Goodwin,** who all generously took time for individual interviews regarding the two Komodo dragons at the Cincinnati Zoo as well as sharing their impressive "dragon file" with the authors. Dr. Maruska and Johnny Arnett also reviewed two drafts of the book and loaned us slides of their trips to Komodo Island and Indonesian zoos. **Michael Dulaney,** Area Supervisor of Cats and Primates, shared his slides of the nesting behavior of the zoo's female dragon. **Charlene** and **Jane** helped out as well.

Peter Strimple of the Herpetological Society of Greater Cincinnati devoted himself to an intense scrutiny of the galleys, ensuring that our quotations and scientific references were in order, for which we owe him great thanks.

Marvin Jones, long associated with the San Diego Zoo, granted us permission to cite his comprehensive document about the history of Komodo dragons in captivity.

Alan I. Kaplan, Naturalist at the Tilden Nature Area in Berkeley, California, was enthusiastic in his support and in providing information about the largest Komodo dragon ever recorded, which is mounted and on display at the park.

Dr. Donald Bruning, Chairman of the American Association of Zoological Parks and Aquariums, **Stephen R. Edwards,** Coordinator of the Species Survival Programme of the International Union for the Conservation of Nature (also known as the World Conservation Union), and **Yoshio Kaneko,** Special Projects Coordinator for the Convention on International Trade in Endangered Species of Wild Fauna and Flora (CITES), all generously allowed their brains to be picked.

Alan Robinson of the U.S. National Park Service reviewed two drafts and made many helpful comments and additions, particularly to the section on The Future of Komodo National Park.

Jim Butler contributed useful ideas.

Dr. Walter Auffenberg of the University of Florida, along with his publisher, the University Presses of Florida, is thanked for permitting us to quote from *The Behavioral Ecology of the Komodo Monitor.* The present book would not have been nearly as accurate and comprehensive without his landmark research.

Michael Pemberton and **Judy Algozin** provided thoughtful reviews of the galleys, helping us with final organizational decisions.

Thanks are also due for the wonderful assistance provided by several staff members of the Salem Public Library, particularly **Mary Finnegan** and **Conrad Pfeiffer** and to **Mary Stuart,** reference librarian at the University of Illinois in Urbana-Champaign, who looked over the galleys and provided expert advice. **Bonnie Irwin** gave additional copyediting suggestions.

Several Indonesians played a part in the creation of this book: **Anwar Duriat,** the guide who invited Dick and Mary Lutz into the dragon's feeding arena on Komodo Island, and **Simon Abady,** the captain of the fishing boat which sailed to Rinca and Komodo. A pleasant and helpful man, Simon is the son of **Nourdin Abady,** who was one of the guides for Dr. Auffenberg.

Closer to home travel agent **Caryn Hainsworth** very efficiently made arrangements for the trip to Indonesia and **April Munks,** Dimi Press assistant, provided excellent service in typing some of the manuscript and performing various other chores.

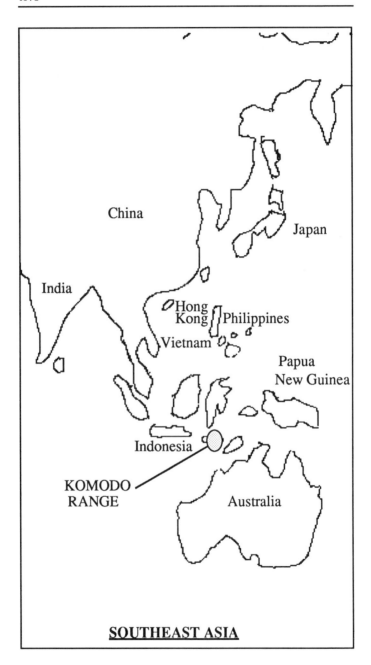

China

Japan

India

Hong
Kong   Philippines

Vietnam

Papua
New Guinea

Indonesia

KOMODO
RANGE   Australia

<u>SOUTHEAST ASIA</u>

CONFRONTATION

Cameras in hand, my wife, Mary, and I stood in the feeding arena within view of a dozen voracious predators. Rangers hang a fresh-killed goat above the gully on Komodo Island every Sunday, but because this was a Tuesday, no bait had been provided. The ranger had suggested we could enter the open end of the untamed reptiles' feeding zone to take a closer look, and we agreed without reservations. (I learned later that the rangers have been asked not to continue this dangerous practice.)

As I crouched and focused my zoom lens on an approaching carnivore, small serrated teeth gleamed in the gaping mouth of the gigantic, dusty-brown lizard. Already I was wondering if I had been foolhardy to enter the arena. The monitor seemed so close that I lowered the camera to judge the distance and discovered, with a gasp, that the nine-foot-long (2.7 m) Komodo dragon was less than five yards (4.5 m) away and closing fast.

I stood and backed up quickly, but in my haste I tripped over a rock behind me and sprawled on the ground. A photograph I had seen that very day flashed through my mind — a six-year-old boy killed by a Komodo dragon, his chest and thighs ripped open in bloody wounds. While preparing to visit this remote Indonesian island, I had read of at least six people attacked by these dangerous lizards, all of whom had either bled to death or died from septic infections. The voice of a fellow tourist heard minutes before echoed in my ears, exclaiming that Komodo dragons can run 20 miles (32 km) an hour.

Mary looked on frozen with fear, her camera forgotten in her hands. Quickly, the ranger stepped forward and warded away the giant monitor with his Y-shaped "dragon stick". As I scrambled to my feet and retreated to safety, I was keenly aware of the gaps in my knowledge about Komodo dragons, the largest lizards in the world. I had begun studying the species before we left the United States, but now I had just faced a dragon in the wild — and was not sure whether I had been in real danger.

I later discovered that Komodo dragons cannot move faster than about 10 miles (16 km) per hour, half the speed I had feared. (Auffenberg, 1981) The lizards I saw in the Komodo Island feeding arena are accustomed to people approaching either while they are eating or afterwards, although most tourists watch from the fenced-off viewing stand on the cliff above the gully. Because Komodo dragons prefer scavenging to killing fresh prey, they do not usually assault people. An adult human armed with a stout stick can turn away an inquisitive Komodo dragon, as our ranger had demonstrated.

Still, the risks involved were real, as were reports of dragon attacks in the past. A person who wanders alone into a hungry dragon's hunting range is in danger, especially if the human is a child, lies down on the ground, or allows the dragon within a yard (.9 m) — close enough for a quick charge. Mary, the ranger, and I had entered the feeding range of these gigantic monitor lizards when no other food was in view. Perhaps some of them had wandered down out of the hills, not having eaten recently and near starvation. Had we known more about the vast appetites and hunting habits of Komodo dragons in the wild, we would certainly have been more cautious.

This first- hand experience emphasized for us how little most people know about the Komodo dragon. As my daughter J. Marie and I continued researching and writing this book, layer after layer of misinformation peeled away. Once exaggerations about size, speed, and even life span were set aside and the myths about its ancestry and lineage were exposed, the Komodo dragon was revealed to us as a unique phenomenon — the world's largest land-dwelling reptile. It is confined to a handful of tiny Indonesian islands and hemmed in by human expansion — balanced in a narrow environmental niche.

Of course, individual Komodo dragons should be treated cautiously and with respect. More than that, the entire species deserves respect from its human neighbors, because the future of these 5,000 giants lies entirely within human hands. We are all responsible for protecting and preserving this species which, like so many others, is endangered by civilization as well as by nature.

Dick Lutz

1

DRAGONS — MYTH AND REALITY

"But I thought dragons weren't real, Mom," one puzzled child said, looking at the Komodo dragons in the Cincinnati Zoo. The response is more than a child's confusion; adults unfamiliar with the Komodo dragon ask the same question when told the subject of this book. The Komodo dragon -- or monitor -- and two other extraordinary lizard species remind humans of the mythical creatures and therefore are named after them. *Draco*, the flying dragon of Malaysia, has skin as brightly colored as a tropical butterfly and fantastic rib-wings that can fold shut like umbrellas or spread wide to help the lizard glide from tree to tree in search of insect prey. The crested dragon, an Australian native, is one of the few lizards that can run on its hind feet; it calls to mind images of the smaller bipedal dinosaurs. Despite their unusual "dragonish" characteristics, both the flying dragon and the crested dragon lack the most mythical characteristic of the Komodo dragon: its great size. All 20 species of *Draco* grow no larger than 8 to 12 inches (20 to 30 cm), much of which is tail, and the full-grown crested dragon is also smaller than a newly-hatched Komodo dragon.

"I had no idea lizards grew so big," wondered a woman as she gazed at the 7-or 8-foot (2.1 or 2.4 m) Komodo dragon replica in Chicago's Field Museum of Natural History. When even a captive dragon or a copy of a mounted specimen causes surprise and disbelief in a safe display behind glass, it is understandable that exaggerated tales of horror would result from encounters in the wild.

Like the Gila "monster" and the horned "toad," the Komodo monitor's popular name owes more to fantasy than to fact, although perhaps the anonymous reporter for a 1926 Berlin newspaper article invented the best title: Drachenparadie (dragon parody or fake dragon). Perhaps there is a bit of Indiana Jones in everyone, ready to believe that the Holy Grail—or dragons—really exist. Although Komodo monitors are not actually dragons, they could be called the closest living relative of the mythical beast: some writers even propose the theory that the Far Eastern, fire-breathing dragon of legend derives from the yellow-tongued Komodo monitor. It is possible that — like the myth of mermaids, which supposedly developed after sailors saw human-like manatees in strange waters — the traditional Chinese dragon has its basis in travelers' tales of Komodo dragons.

> Surprisingly speedy, keen of eye and nose, they are the fiercest lizard known; having long yellow-orange tongues, they may have inspired the mythical Chinese dragons (Porter, 1972).

Birth of a Belief

Humans have lived in Indonesia since at least 40,000 B.C., as artifacts found in the region prove. Historians believe that relations between the people of the

Indian subcontinent and the Malay archipelago (including modern Indonesia) date back to prehistory (Toussaint, 1966).

In fact, between 3000 and 500 B.C., Mongol immigrants from what is now China brought Stone, Bronze, and Iron Age cultures and languages to the Malay Islands north of Indonesia. Evidence of Chinese influence in Indonesia can be traced to thousands of years ago, and Komodo expert Walter Auffenberg (1981) believes archeological data indicate that human contact with Komodo monitors may be equally ancient.

It is therefore possible that embellished accounts of the "dragons of Komodo" were carried to China before the legend of the fire-breathing dragon first occurred there in the third century A.D. In literature, the Chinese imperial dragon may be traced to the Wu dynasty of 222-227 A.D (Minton and Minton, 1973).

> The ebb and flow of trade, for the centuries preceding the steamship and aeroplane, were determined by the monsoon and trade winds. The Indonesian islands, and the Malay archipelago, provided a convenient midway point where the merchants of the civilized world met and exchanged goods. They also, with less awareness of what was happening, exchanged ideas (Zainu'ddin, 1970).

To assume, based on this contact between cultures and beliefs, that an Indonesian lizard was the inspiration for the Chinese dragon legend may seem far-fetched, but it should be noted that the spread of major religions to Indonesia took a similar route. During the first few centuries A.D., Hindu priests and traders spread their culture and religion throughout Indonesia, while a Buddhist kingdom sprang up on Sumatra, brought to the island either from its original home in India or through Chinese influence, and lasted from the seventh through the 14th centuries A.D. According to Auguste Tousssaint (1966), Chinese navigators did not visit the Malay region before the fifth century A.D. but contact between the two cultures dates to much earlier times.

> [I]t is clear that, from very early times, China had important diplomatic and commercial connections with southeast Asia. The bulk of the early trade between Indonesian islands and China was probably initiated by Indonesians and carried on in Indonesian ships. The Chinese reports seem secondhand, probably from information provided by envoys in tribute-bearing missions. This allowed plenty of scope for misunderstanding, vagueness and misinformation (Zainu'ddin, 1970).

An account survives of a Chinese traveler of 414 A.D. who was returning to China from the Indonesian area in a large merchant ship carrying 200 men. They sailed in fear of pirates and were caught in storms, during which unnamed monsters were seen.

> In the darkness of the night, only the great waves were to be seen breaking on one another and emitting a brightness like that of fire, with large turtles and other monsters of the deep [all about]... The sea was deep and bottomless and there was no place they could drop anchor (Legge, 1886).

Although Komodo dragons swim only short distances between islands and would not have been among these "monsters of the deep", the story is an example of the early rumors that caused the uncharted regions of maps to be labeled "Here there be dragons."

Dragons Throughout Time

Is it possible that the huge monitor lizards from a sprinkling of small Indonesian islands could have been the source of the Chinese dragon myth, which was first recorded in the heart of China countless miles to the north? Given the extent of trade and cultural exchange recorded above, it must be accepted as possible. But is it likely?

If a single reptile type directly influenced the creation of the myth, it is much more probable that the Chinese dragon was based on the large, four-footed, carnivorous reptiles known throughout the region — the crocodilians. Of the 13 crocodilian species in the eastern hemisphere, the five-foot-long (1.5 m) alligator of eastern China is closest to the source of the myth, and several authors suspect it of being the "more probable prototype of the dragon" (Pope, 1955). Apparently, the Chinese used to display alligators at fairs, billing them as dragons (Work Projects Administration, 1939).

> The land and water dragons that permeate the culture of China, Korea, and Japan were doubt-less based on the alligator of China, but behind this comparatively small and innocuous croc-odilian glides the shadow of the great beast that lurked along the southern coasts of old China, the saltwater crocodile (Minton and Minton, 1973).

Perhaps it can be deduced that the mythical Eastern dragon was based on rumors about the Chinese alligator, but that as time passed and the legends grew, attributes of the huge saltwater crocodile, which ranges from southeast Asia to India to northern Australia, were also given to the monstrous legend. *Crocodylus porosus* has been recorded at lengths of 13 to 19 feet (4 to 5.8 m) and may grow as long as 28 feet (8.4 m), but even a much smaller specimen can be deadly to humans. Both the saltwater crocodile and the Nile crocodile (which the Mintons believe may have been the source of the European dragon legend) are well known for killing and eating humans. In *Dangerous to Man*, RogerCaras (1975) reported that the saltwater crocodile may even be more dangerous to people than sharks.

Rumors and legends about the Komodo monitors — circulated after the Chinese myth originated — may well have helped reinforce belief in dragons through later generations. The flickering yellow tongue of the giant Komodo lizard, which is unique in the lizard family, might well explain the fire-breathing aspect of the Chinese dragon. Dr. Auffenberg (1981) feels it is reasonably certain that Komodo dragons and their skins were traded with the Chinese as long ago as the 1100s, just about the time the submerged Indonesian culture reasserted itself and rejected Hinduism.

The city of Ujung Padang on the island of Sulawesi lies due north of Komodo across the Java Sea, a distance of 280 miles (452 km). The Ujung Padang region is still home to the Bugis and Makasarese, tribes known historically as Sea Gypsies — the most feared pirates of the Java Sea. For centuries, Bugis (the source of the English term "boogyman") traded with many countries, including China, and were known as skilled navigators. The cast-bronze bows of their ships, designed to ram into other vessels, were shaped like scaled dragons' gullets, an image that may have been based on the Chinese legend — or on rumors from a nearer source about the living dragons of Komodo.

2

DISCOVERY

As the twentieth century dawned, the American West had been civilized for a decade, but new explorations, discoveries, and scientific wonders were being unveiled every day. On 4 July 1899, Wyoming fossil-hunters financed by the millionaire Andrew Carnegie uncovered the first complete dinosaur skeleton to be found in the New World: an 84-foot-long (25.9 m) *Diplodocus*. In 1901, Theodore Roosevelt began eight years as the United States president, and his mania for traveling the great outdoors, hunting and exploring, set the tone for the national mood. In two more years, the age of air travel would begin.

Half a world away, north of Australia and south of China, United States forces had just helped to liberate the Spanish colony of the Philippine Islands; by 1901, the country was officially United States property. Soldiers returning home must have fascinated their neighbors and friends with descriptions of this warm, wet, tropical land. Seven thousand inhabited islands and rocks in the area belonged to the Philippines, while additional thousands to the south were part of the Dutch East Indies colony. Now the independent Republic of Indonesia, the country includes the Greater Sunda Islands to the west and the little-known Lesser Sunda Islands to the east. Looking at his map, the U.S. veteran could point to a few of the Greater Sunda Islands whose names were already vaguely familiar to westerners, larger islands such as Sumatra, Java, Borneo, and the smaller Bali.

No one in the region or the world took special notice of a few small, mostly uninhabited islands east of Bali and south of Borneo, for the world at large did not yet know of the 9-to 10-foot-long (2.8 to 3.1 m) reptilian carnivores that ruled three of the Lesser Sunda Islands and intruded on four others. It was true that rumors had surfaced from time to time of some huge monster in that area of the archipelago. According to Minton and Minton, traders and fishermen returning from the Sundas told of a *boeaja darat* (now spelled *buaya darat*), a "land crocodile," supposedly reaching lengths of up to 20 feet (6.1 m) and able to pull down a water buffalo. Another story told how pearl divers washed ashore on Komodo Island during a storm had encountered fantastic beasts with enormous claws, fearsome teeth, heavily armored bodies, and fiery yellow tongues. The Dutch who controlled the region may have scoffed at these tales, if they even heard them, as the Abominable Snowmen or Loch Ness monsters of their time.

A later version of the first Western contact with the monitor lizards of Komodo sounds like the plot of an action-adventure movie: supposedly, an airplane crash-landed on Komodo Island in 1910, and the Dutch pilot returned to Java reporting that he had seen one or more huge lizards at least 13 feet (4 m) long.

> To add to his already considerable difficulties
> with primitive equipment, he found to his dismay
> that he had also to contend with these enormous

reptiles that prowled hungrily around the wreckage of his plane. (Watson, 1987)

Like many other anecdotes about Komodo dragons, a kernel of truth has been embellished with layers of myth, and respectable authors find themselves unintentionally repeating unproved rumors as if they were facts. In this case, it seems probable that the Dutch airman of 1910 was actually the English aviator Cobham who arrived in Bima on the Lesser Sunda Island of Sumbawa in 1926 and encountered a captive Komodo dragon there, almost two decades after the animals' official entry into scientific listings. There is documentation of Cobham's visit — his letter to the *London Times*, which caused quite a stir. No original source for the Dutch airman story has ever been found (Jones, 1965).

At any rate, just as modern scientists refuse to believe in flying saucer sightings until they have proof, the gigantic lizards of Komodo were not accepted as real until they had been seen and studied by a reputable scientist.

Scientific Verification

The Komodo dragons' transition from regional phenomenon to scientific acknowledgment began in December, 1910, with First Lieutenant J. K. H. van Steyn van Hensbroek, a civil administrator stationed in Reo on the north central coast of Flores, a large, well-populated Lesser Sunda Island. Inhabitants had told him about a huge "land crocodile" that lived on the western-most coast near the town of Laboean Badjo (now spelled Labuan Bajo or Labuhanbajo) and on small nearby Komodo Island. When his tour of duty took him to Komodo, the soldier found the island was an old volcanic spur jutting up from the ocean between Flores and Sumbawa, its mountains and plains now covered with grasslands, brush, and forest. Fauna ranged in size from deer and water buffalo to mice. The only permanent human inhabitants, then as now, lived in Kampung Komodo (Komodo Village) on Telok Slawi (Python Bay) on the eastern coast of the 22- by 12-mile (35-by 19-km) island. According to a 1928 visitor, the community consisted of 40 convicts exiled by the Sultan of Sumbawa (Burden, 1928).

Two hunters, Kock and Aldegon, members of the Dutch pearling fleet in the area, confirmed the animals' existence; Aldegon said he had even shot a few before the number of island visitors increased and the giant lizards began withdrawing into the mountains. The men estimated that the hunter's larger kills may have been as long as 20 or 23 feet (6.1 or 7 m), although there were no skins or other remains to prove they were of such extraordinary size.

Lieutenant van Steyn van Hensbroek killed a Komodo dragon measuring about 7 feet (2.1 m) in length and sent a photograph and the skin to Major P. A. Ouwens, director of the Zoological Museum and Botanical Gardens in Buitenzorg (now called Bogor), Java, who took on the responsibility of scientifically verifying the story (Ouwens, 1912). The museum director sent an Indonesian collector to join the soldier in trying to catch a larger, living specimen. Lieutenant van Steyn van Hensbroek had warned Major Ouwens that the project would be difficult "as the inhabitants will not run the risk, for the animals not only bite, but keep the natives at a respectful distance by powerful blows with their tails." By the time the museum collector arrived on Komodo, Lieutenant van Steyn van Hensbroek had been transferred south to Timor Island, so the collector recruited the Raja Bitjara (now spelled Bicara, the native chief or rajah) and "the necessary natives and dogs" to help in the hunt. They bagged two adults measuring nearly 10 feet and 7 feet, 9 inches (3.1 and 2.35 m) respectively and captured two live youngsters about three feet (.9 m) long.

Realizing the so-called "land crocodile" was actually a monitor lizard, Major Ouwens named the new species *Varanus komodoensis* and published his findings for the scientific community. In full scientific terminology, the lizard is called *Varanus komodoensis* Ouwens to identify the scientist as well as the species. His article included a description of the Komodo dragons in the wild, based on the lieutenant's notes and corroborated by the collector.

> They live...exclusively on land, where they make great holes under the stones and rocks, in which they always remain at night. Their feet are fairly long, and in spite of their awkward build, they can move with great rapidity.
>
> In walking, they do not touch the ground, neither with the chest nor with the belly. They walk on the balls of the feet, as may be clearly seen by the callosities on them, as well as by their footprints. The neck is rather long and extraordinarily mobile. The animal can move its head in every direction, and so it can see everything: this is of great use to the creature, as it seems to be remarkably deaf. [This claim was later disproved] They live either singly or in troops. Their food is exclusively of animal nature (Ouwens, 1912).

The Largest Living Land Reptile

Monitors are among the most streamlined of lizards, unadorned by neck ruffles, back spines, or elaborate bumps or horns. Like most adult monitors, the full-grown Komodo dragon has a dull color pattern; it is brownish grey or reddish grey except for its yellow forked tongue. In some adult dragons, the legs and head are clearly blacker than the body and tail. Every monitor lizard has a distinctive, darting forked tongue, which is so long that — unlike the tongues of other lizards — it retracts into a sheath on the floor of the mouth when it is not in use. The Komodo dragon's teeth are ideally adapted for grasping and tearing flesh, bearing a greater resemblance to the teeth of sharks than to those of other reptiles or mammals.

Comparing the Komodo dragon with other lizards naturally raises the question of its size, and in fact, this is often the first question asked by the general public: how large does it get? The longest possible length for a Komodo dragon was under dispute for many years, especially since the huge beasts had never been measured. This fascination with length has led scientific expeditions to make careful records of the lengths of all captured and killed dragons. Among the unconfirmed stories are several told to Lieutenant van Steyn van Hensbroek: Aldegon's tale of a 20-to 23-foot-long (6.1 or 7 m) gargantua was followed by a report that a soldier named Sergeant Beker had shot a 13-foot-long (4 m) Komodo dragon. A later version (Burden, 1928) described Sergeant Beker claiming his longest dragon was 11 feet, 9 inches (3.6 m), but none of the above stories was verified by physical evidence or photographs.

The longest Komodo dragon ever measured was a giant 365-pound (165.9 kg) specimen 10 feet, 2.5 inches (3.13 m) long. The behemoth died in the St. Louis Zoo in 1933; it was stuffed and is currently on display at Tilden Regional Park near Berkeley, California.

The 23-foot-long (7 meter) *buaya darat* rumored in Major Ouwens' day was a legend born of reality and fear combined. However, it is entirely likely that, as with fishing, "the biggest ones got away,"and some Komodo dragons in the wild may well have reached 10 feet, 6 inches or 11 feet (3.2 or 3.36 m.). Zoologists generally state that the giant lizard reaches lengths "up to" ten feet, though Dr. Auffenberg (1981) the only herpetologist who has extensively studied the species, finds a more typical size for adult Komodo dragons is no longer than 8 feet, 6 inches (2.6 m) and approximately 119 pounds (54 kg).

A recent book (Adams and Carwardine, 1990) claims that a monitor now living on Komodo "is over twelve feet long [3.7 m] and stands about a yard [.9 m] high", but the measurement of the large dragon, which the authors may not have seen personally, is more likely an estimate: no other sources refer to a dragon of that size currently known on the island. A number of sources refer to dragons as "12-foot monsters," but the origin of this measurement may simply be zoo keepers' or zoologists' estimates that dragons in the wild may be capable of reaching 12 feet (3.7 m) in length.

While some monitor species are more slender, the Komodo dragon, at least in adulthood, has a heavy build with sturdy legs, a long thick neck, a thick tail, and even a wide, alligator-like snout. An 8-foot-long (2.4 meter) *Varanus komodoensis* is a hefty and formidable specimen. If it were placed in a cage with a Malayan water monitor (*V. salvator*) of the same length, the Komodo dragon would obviously be the heavier of the two. Actually putting members of the two different species in the same enclosure would not be wise, however: the experiment was tried by the Washington, D.C., Zoo in 1964, and within two months the dragon attacked the water monitor, seizing it by the throat and rendering it helpless until keepers intervened. The water monitor later died (DePrato, "Twentieth Century Dragons").

Several sources state that the long but more slender Salvador's monitors (*V. salvadorii*)may grow longer than the longest known Komodo dragon, perhaps as long as 14 or 15 feet (4.2 or 4.5 m) (Worrell, 1967; Auffenberg, 1981; Strimple, 1990). Drs. Worrell and Auffenberg add, however, that absolute documentation has not been provided. Should the rumors prove to be true, the Komodo dragon can still lay claim to being the world's largest lizard, because it would be only the length of the other monitor's tail that enabled it to break the record. The Salvador's monitor's tail is much longer than its head and body combined, while the Komodo dragon's tail is only half of its total length.

The Komodo dragon's head is also taller and its snout much broader, so that a lay person comparing the skulls of the three monitor species might at first think the dragon's skull was that of an alligator and the other two monitors' skulls those of snakes. In fact, although casual viewers at zoos have been known to confuse the two, dragons are not at all closely related to the crocodilians. The confusion is doubtlessly based primarily on the lizard's large size; Dr. Worrell reports that New Guinea natives call Salvador's monitor a "tree-dwelling crocodile" (Worrell, 1967), just as Komodo natives call the Komodo dragon a "land crocodile."

The Early Years

Lieutenant van Steyn van Hensbroek, although told by natives that Komodo dragons inhabited southwestern Flores, had no opportunity to explore further before his transfer. Soon after Major Ouwens's official announcement of the species' existence, another Dutch expedition killed and skinned a Komodo dragon near Labuan Bajo on western Flores, providing an 8-foot, 9-inch long (2.68 m) skin and skull for the Leyden Museum in the Netherlands. "Miss Dr." Nelly de Rooij (also spelled "de Rooy") analyzed the artifacts obtained by the expedition and was able to expand on Major Ouwens's scientific observations about the species in her 1915 study of the reptiles of the Malay Archipelago (de Jong, 1927; Dunn, 1927a; Burden, 1928).

What a flurry of excitement there must have been among zoologists — not to mention big game hunters — when the Komodo dragons' existence was proved to the world. But Major Ouwens' timing was unfortunate; World War I soon exploded into the headlines and for five years every nation's energy was turned to the front lines of the largest war the world had ever seen. Other than inspecting the Komodo dragon skin and skull in the Leyden Museum, European scientists had few opportunities to study the new species in the decade after its scientific discovery. In the meantime, both native and Dutch rulers had declared it illegal to hunt dragons for sport, and limited the number that could be collected for scientific study or for zoos.

As the war neared its end, collection of the Komodo monitors resumed, although it was to be several years before anyone attempted to catch more live dragons. In 1923, Duke Adolf Friedrich von Mecklenburg killed four dragons, the smaller three of which were exhibited in the Buitenzorg Museum along with the largest of Major Ouwens's specimens. The fourth Mecklenburg trophy, nearly 10 feet (3 m) long, was mounted in the Berlin Museum (Dunn, 1927a).

Because Komodo dragons were known to inhabit both Komodo Island and the western coast of Flores, in 1924 O. Horst explored Komodo, Mbora (now called Gili Morong) off the western tip of Flores, and the almost-Komodo-sized island which lay between the other two islands: Rinca. The island's name has also been spelled Rindja, Rintja, and Rinja, but is always pronounced REEN-cha. O. Horst logically assumed that Rinca would be part of the dragons' range, and in fact herpetologist Emmett Reid Dunn (1927a) reported that the Dutchman shot and killed a dragon there that measured just under 6-foot, 7-inches (2 m). The Horst expedition's visits to Flores and Rinca established the dragons' range to be wider than was previously known.

O. Horst may have been the source for the live dragon that the aviator Cobham encountered chained to a tree in Bima, before it was brought to the Amsterdam Zoological Garden at the end of 1926. Proof of the species' predatory nature was obtained when this dragon jumped on an old pony that had strayed within reach and lacerated the horse so badly that it had to be shot (Burden, 1928). By the time the then-tame dragon arrived in the Netherlands, it "was in a rather bad condition", Dr. de Jong explained (1927). He studied the animal after its death and was able to expand on Dr. de Rooij's observations, publishing two scientific articles about the external characteristics and internal organization of the skeleton.

The Public Discovers Komodo Dragons

Enter an imaginary New York movie house in 1926 just as the Pathe newsreel begins. In world news, Emperor Hirohito and Benito Mussolini have become leaders of their nations; the entertainment report announces that silent movie heartthrob Rudolph Valentino has died. Then perhaps, just before the movie starts, there is a light feature about a great zoological adventure—the first American expedition to Komodo Island has been launched and the New York Zoological Park (the Bronx Zoo) is preparing a cage for its new inhabitants.

"Komodo Island, by an act of the Dutch Colonial Government, is a game preserve," W. Douglas Burden, the expedition's organizer and leader, later reported. "Thanks to the Governor General of the Dutch East Indies, we were given permission to secure fifteen specimens" (Burden, 1928).

The expedition was a herpetologist's dream; the group visited eight islands, including Java and Bali, and Dr. Dunn collected 249 lizards of 27 species (four were previously unknown to the scientific world) and three subspecies.   However, the focus of the expedition was the Komodo dragon.   Members of the expedition found dragon tracks on Padar Island between Komodo and Rinca, thus increasing once more the known range of the dragons. The species' total range was now known: about 345 square miles (894 square km), one-quarter the size of Rhode Island, an area including many square miles of ocean between the islands. The primary concentration was on the dragons of Komodo Island.

In the Introduction to his [Douglas Burden's] popular book on the expedition, one is told (Marvin Jones questions this account, indicating that the trip was planned after a visit to Berlin where Burden learned about the dragon and how to get to Komodo Island) that the idea of a dragon hunting trip came suddenly one evening at his home in New York and that in quick order a professional herpetologist, a Pathe cameraman, and a skilled hunter were rounded up and the exploration initiated.... "Thus they set off in a blaze of publicity, and returned later in the year with the first live Komodo Dragon[s] to reach a public zoological garden, and reams of credits in newspapers throughout the globe, ably assisted by Pathe news" (Jones, 1964).

During their four-week stay on the island, Douglas Burden and Dr. Dunn were able to develop a fairly accurate picture of the dragons in their native environment. Using slaughtered wild pigs as bait, the expedition captured 19 of the dragons, which usually roam the open woodlands, feeding on deer, pigs, water buffalo, birds, and eggs.   Five dragons were released together on a beach as an experiment and, while two ran into the jungle, three escaped into the water and swam under the surface until they were out of the humans' range before returning to the island (Burden, 1928).

> According to the natives, wild horses are plentiful on the island of Rindja where they form the chief food supply of the giant lizard. ...On Padar, the lizards live almost entirely on turtle eggs which they dig up on the beaches. This was determined from the droppings which often contained undigested remains of egg shells. ... They are so voracious that they will eat any rotten meat including that of their own kind. If one of their number is wounded, it is subject to attack (Burden, 1928).

The largest male dragon they measured was 9 feet, 2 inches (2.8 m), and the longest female was 6 feet, 6 inches (2 m). Douglas Burden and Dr. Dunn both felt that the earlier reports of Aldegon, Koch and Sergeant. Beker must have been "utterly inaccurate." Douglas Burden also noted that the species "avoids man but reacts only to visual stimuli"; members of the expedition were able to hide behind blinds and watch the dragons, even filming one killing and eating a goat tethered nearby as bait. Like Major Ouwens before him, Douglas Burden at first thought the species was deaf but he later learned that dragons in the London Zoo would respond to sounds that meant they were about to be fed (Burden, 1928).
One day, when Mrs. Burden had set aside her gun, she was cornered by a Komodo dragon in the wild; at the last minute, the party's professional hunter shot and killed the approaching monitor. Her story, in vivid and occasionally inaccurate prose (she called the monitors "shaggy"), is a clear warning of the difference between wild dragons and the tamer zoo variety.

[He] approached step by step, the great bulk of
his body held clear of the ground...the black
beady eyes flashing in their deep sockets... A
hoary customer, black as dead lava... Occas-
sionally, ...he stopped and raised himself on
those iron forelegs to look around. ...

Nearer he came and nearer...with grim head
swinging heavily from side to side. I remem-
bered all the fantastic stories I had heard of
these creatures attacking both men and horses,
and was in no wise reassured. Now listening
to the short hissing that came like a gust of evil
wind, and observing the action of that darting, snake-like tongue, that seemed to sense
the very fear that held me, I was affected in a
manner not easy to relate. ...

The creature was now less than five yards away,
and its subtle reptilian smell was in my nostrils.
Too late to leap from hiding-if I did, he would
surely spring upon me, rending me and devour-
ing my remains as he had devoured the dead
deer. Better to take my chances where I lay, so
I closed my eyes and waited (Burden, 1927a).

Pathe, which later merged with Metro Goldwyn
Mayer and became MGM-Pathe Communications, provided exclusive coverage of the expedition and gave the
Burdens valuable publicity; it was the equivalent of two
recent modern expeditions with television camera crews
which became the basis of PBS's *The Ring of Fire* and of a
National Geographic special. The glory of being first and
the film shot by the Pathe cameraman earned the expedition worldwide news coverage. The Burdens brought
back two living monitors for the Bronx Zoo, and the

remainder of the dragons were dissected for scientific study or stuffed and mounted for an exhibit in the Hall of Reptiles at the American Museum of Natural History in Washington, D.C. This exhibit still exists. The two live dragons at the Bronx Zoo — the first ever seen in the New World—brought in crowds of curiosity seekers, although both dragons died within two months.

The adventure yielded sufficient material for Dr. Dunn to write several scientific articles about Komodo Island reptiles and for Douglas Burden to write three articles and a book. *Dragon Lizards of Komodo* was the first general interest book about the Komodo monitors, and Douglas Burden's term for *V. komodoensis* became its popular name: the Komodo dragon. The in-depth study of the giant lizards in their own environment provided valuable new information; in fact, many introductory books on reptiles in libraries and book stores today still base most of their Komodo dragon sections on the discoveries of this 1926 expedition.

Between the Burden expedition and Asia's participation in World War II, a number of other scientific studies of the dragons were made, even as governmental protection of the species was more strictly enforced. Einar Lonnberg (1928) pointed out that dragons were brought to the United States and Europe "in so great a number that material for the study of the same has become available to zoologists." Dr. Lonnberg himself based his study on the skin and skull of a dragon loaned by the Amsterdam Zoological Museum, the same institution that had allowed Dr. de Jong to study the remains of another dead dragon.

Collection expeditions continued, with Dutch and U.S. collectors among the most numerous, although not all expeditions were documented. For example, Chicago's Field Museum of Natural History features a cellulose-acetate reproduction of a dragon captured by the Chancellor-Stuart expedition of 1929, but no written record of the expedition was found while this book was being researched.

In 1933, a fictional account of a South Seas exploration thrilled movie audiences across the country, with the horrifying King Kong rendering audiences stiff with fear. As if it were a continuation of the fictional adventure film, two American collectors the same year returned from Indonesia with the largest dragon ever measured — a 10 foot, 2.5 inch (3.13 m) giant that drew thousands of visitors to the St. Louis Zoo. Unfortunately, the dragon had caught pneumonia during the long ocean voyage, and it died two weeks after going on display.

In 1936 a group of English adventurers combined their safari yearnings with the London Zoo's collection needs. A popular pair of dragons had been provided to the zoo the year after the Burden expedition, but one of them had died several years later. Arriving at Komodo Island aboard Lord Moyne's yacht, the party spent ten days on the island and managed to capture seven dragons. Due to the limitations of their export permit, the British collectors brought only three dragons aboard the yacht. One promptly escaped and was presumed to have slipped overboard and swum away.

Lady Broughton was the party's chronicler, and her photographs and story were published in the September 1936 issue of *National Geographic*. Looking at the Komodo monitor, Lady Broughton saw a monster out of legends and the mists of time.

> [I]ts great size and general appearance...vividly suggests the fire-breathing dragon of legend. Perhaps such a reptile, with curling tail [monitors curl their tails sideways and then strike at attackers] and long, forked, flame-like tongue, for thousands of years inspired Chinese artists in picturing the traditional dragon (Broughton, 1936).

The Modern Komodo Dragon

In the aftermath of World War II, study of Komodo dragons continued on an international basis, with a number of scientific expeditions making additional discoveries. In the summer of 1953, herpetologist A. Hoogerwerf visited Komodo, Rinca, and little-known Padar over a 1 1/2 month period, observing how dragons eat carrion in groups. Three years later, Dr. P. Pfeffer and other French zoologists studied dragons on Komodo, Rinca, and Flores and discovered that, although the lizards roam after sunset, humans seldom see them because their eyes do not reflect light. I.S. Darevskii and S. Kadarsan (1964) led the Indonesian-Soviet expedition of 1962, which spent about a month on Komodo, Rinca, and Padar, focusing on such details as body temperature, feeding habits, and propagation. At the time, dragons were still considered so numerous that the expedition was allowed to kill and dissect three adult dragons to determine details about their reproductive systems. They found that the female had laid eggs about a month earlier.

By the late 1960's, the scientific and zoological world had developed an increasing concern about the survival potential of the Komodo dragon. Only 1,100 dragons were believed to remain in the wild, which would indicate that the dragon was an endangered species on the brink of extinction. In 1968, the New York Zoological Society funded an expedition to "determine if enough monitors remain there to warrant a major study of their behavior and ecology." F. Wayne King, reptile curator for the Bronx Zoo, and photographer James Kern were in many ways retracing the steps of Douglas Burden and Dr. Dunn, though in the intervening years the focus of zoological societies had changed to more conservationist concerns. If it were still possible to save the dragons, a complete study of the species in their own

environment would need to be done and a manage
program begun to ensure the species' preservation (
1968).

> So basic a piece of data as the size of the
> animal's home range — necessary for an ac
> rate estimate of the monitor population — i
> lacking. So are details on mating behavior,
> frequency of breeding, number of eggs pro-
> duced, and where the clutch is deposited: tl
> makes it difficult to predict reproductive
> potential. Other important but missing facts
> about the monitors involve their activity cyc
> temperature and humidity requirements, si;
> of young at hatching, growth rate, and the tii
> it takes the lizards to mature. Although it is
> known the animals feed on pig and deer, the
> exact diet is unknown. So is the lizard's
> lifespan (King, 1968).

As a result of Dr. King's report, Walter Auffenbe
a herpetologist from the University of Florida
Gainesville, volunteered to spend a year in field study
Komodo Island. From July, 1969 through June, 1970, L
Auffenberg was able to provide a thorough and accura
scientific study of the Komodo monitor. His resear
included two additional month-long visits, one to Flor
in the summer of 1971, and a return to Komodo in 197
A reader wishing to learn more about the Komodo drago
than is contained in this book cannot do better than to bu
a copy of Dr. Auffenberg's book, *The Behavioral Ecology*
the Komodo Monitor.

This year-long field study of the dragons o
Komodo gave herpetologists and zoo curators a thor
ough basis for understanding the species in their nativ
habitat. Dr. Auffenberg counted more than 300 dragon:

or *oras*, as the natives call them, and monitored the activities of 117 during 1969-1970 , mostly on the island of Komodo itself. He measured their weight and length, tagged them and painted numbers on their sides to identify them after release, harnessed radio transmitters to three to trace their movements, and observed them extensively while hidden behind blinds.

Among other discoveries, Dr. Auffenberg learned the most accurate way of determining a dragon's sex externally is to look for a minute variation in the groin's scale pattern. Using this method, he found adult male dragons outnumber adult females by a ratio of 3.5 to 1 and estimated that there are only about 400 adult females on the island. Based on the population densities in the different regions he examined, he estimated the total number of adult dragons at the time to be 5,713.   Dr. Auffenberg's 1981 book forms the basis of much of the next chapter.

Komodo dragons in the wild

Komodo dragon in captivity

Photo courtesy of Michael Dulaney

3

THE LIFE OF THE DRAGON

If some dragon-detecting radar were developed and the equipment focused on Komodo Island, several thousand hot spots would dot the 75-square-mile (121 square km) land mass from its mountainous wooded ridges, through the grassy highlands dotted with palms and shade trees and into the forested valleys sloping down toward sandy beaches. Dragon-shaped outlines would appear in burrows where some adults escape from the midday sun. A scan of the 40-foot (12.2 m) tall tamarind trees would show 8-to 24-inch (20.3 to 61 cm) long youngsters hidden in hollows and under bark, the safest place to avoid becoming a larger dragon's dinner. Some dragons might snooze under azyma bushes, where they earlier searched for napping deer or boar. If it were mid-morning or mid-afternoon, most dragons would be roaming through the tropical savannas and monsoon forests in search of prey, living or dead.

The ora is provided with a highly sophisti-
cated neural anatomy, particularly...vision
and olfaction. .... Though optimal body temperatures do not differ significantly from those
of most other reptiles, ...deep body temperatures tend to remain more uniform day and
night throughout the year than they do for
any other reptile in the world. The anatomy
of its circulatory system suggests that there is
less mixing of oxygenated and unoxygenated
blood during its rounds through the body
than there is in any other lizard or snake.
Finally, animal keepers in zoos and animal
behaviorists...seem convinced that it is one of
the most intelligent reptiles in the world
(Auffenberg, 1981).

The ideal way to learn as much as possible about
the dragon lizards of Komodo in a single day, without
hiding behind a blind or relying on a camera, would be to
see them through the eyes of a fellow animal, keen-eyed,
swift-traveling, and comfortable in the extreme heat of an
Indonesian summer day. A monkey might be a good
choice, but there are none left on Komodo, and if one were
imported some tree-climbing adolescent dragon might
make a meal out of it. A better choice would be to enter
the mind of an animal which travels farther, sees more,
and is well-equipped to avoid the jaws of the dragons. A
white-breasted sea eagle is one possibility, but it would
prefer to fish far out at sea, having little interest in the
activities of the land-focused dragons. The bird most
likely to follow dragons is the jungle crow, which also
feeds on carrion.

Begin soaring above the island just before daylight
and watch the animal world of Komodo awaken. A
handful of Rusa deer already graze on a hillside covered

A dragon burrowing

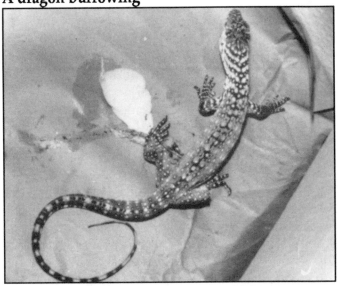

Photo courtesy of Michael Dulaney

A young dragon

Photo courtesy of Surabaya Zoo

with 6-foot-tall (2 m) themeda grasses, a boar snuffles under a thicket of jatropha bushes behind the sand dunes to nap after a busy night, a feral dog trots down a savanna forest path, and a grey and white Pacific reef egret launches itself over the bay where dolphins leap up and manta rays glide in the morning light. In a hillside monsoon forest alive with the crows of wild green jungle fowl, a big-eyed tokay gecko crawls out on the leafless branch of a tamarind tree to warm itself in the early sun. In the dry creek bed below, its gigantic distant relative follows the same urge.

At first only a foot or so (ca. 31 cm) of the dragon's thick reddish tail sticks out of a burrow in the dirt bank, and then the monitor backs slowly out of its den, muscular thighs lifting and pushing the heavy black and pink speckled body backward. Few females grow as long as this 7 foot , 6 inch (2.5 m) specimen, and if it were a full grown dragon of either sex, it would be a duller shade, more brownish-grey or brick-red except for the yellowish-green speckles on its snout. This dragon must be male, then; probably eight to twelve years old, he will continue to grow throughout his life. He has been awake for several hours, lying partially outside the too-small hole after a night spent with his head facing out and his tail curled beside him to allow his whole body to fit inside.

Moving sluggishly, he finds a bowl-shaped basking spot already scratched in the dirt nearby and spreads out to absorb as much sunlight as possible with his stomach flat, black-tinted legs sprawled out on both sides, and dark neck and chin stretched out on the ground, yellow eyelids blinking over dark brown eyes. The dragon has about four of these basking spots, each near a burrow, natural hollow, rockslide or overhanging thicket where he occasionally spends the night. The burrows might be the abandoned holes of other animals, but more likely he dug his own where the ground is soft and forms a slope or angle.

In a day that may last from 4:30 a.m. to 11:30 p.m., this voracious animal — capable of eating an entire boar in a single quick meal—will spend on average only about seven minutes actually eating. The rest of the time will be consumed with searching for prey and interacting with or avoiding others of his species. Like all Komodo dragons, especially the larger ones, he will be interrupted repeatedly by his need to thermoregulate—to increase or reduce his body temperature. After basking in the morning sun until around 9 a.m., he will spend most of the rest of the day, especially after noon or when he has just eaten, trying to cool down. The sunlight is useful to him now, but its searing heat during his hunting hours will frequently force him off the open grasslands and into the shade of the boundary woodlands; at midday, he will drowse for several hours in a cool burrow or under a bush (Auffenberg, 1978).

Although he may sleep in different places from night to night, this dragon is a resident. Half his time is spent within a small core area that provides most of his basic needs — thickets, burrows and rockslides for napping and sleeping in, a few good spots where he can hide to ambush prey, some high ground where he can test the winds for the scent of nearby carrion, several dunging sites where he can mark his territory and a now-dry water hole. One edge of his core area overlaps with that of a female dragon and they have mated several times, but they will probably not meet today unless both are drawn to the same place by the smell of carrion.

Surrounding the dragon's core area is his foraging range, criss-crossed with trails leading him to all the live prey available nearby: incubator mounds built by megapode birds where eggs can be found and parent birds caught, thickets where deer and boar sleep, and even, since he is near the ocean, a section of beach where sea turtles sometimes lay their eggs. Dragons' territories usually include dry monsoon forest and savanna habitats but they touch on mangrove swamps, open beach, steppe, thickets, and even offshore islets, reefs, and bars.

The dragon will pause to leave a dropping before he sets out on his hunting route. Dragons convey a great deal of information to each other with their dung, which is primarily white and left out in the open where other dragons can easily find it. They tongue each dropping they encounter with such intent interest, like dogs picking up messages from communal fire hydrants or telephone poles, that Dr. Auffenberg assumes they are learning about the size, age, and possibly sex and breeding condition of each dragon that has passed along the same trail. Because dragons are such efficient scavenger-predators — and feral dogs, jungle crows, and carrion-eating beetles quickly finish off the few remains of their prey — examination of fecal pellets provides more clues about dragon prey species than searching for carcasses does. Walking to the feeding arena on a Tuesday, Dick and Mary Lutz were shown a fecal pellet which the guide opened, pointing out some hair which he said was from the bait goat that the dragon had eaten on the previous Sunday.

The favorite prey of adult dragons appears to be boar, deer, and other dragons, although when opportunity offers, they will also eat water buffalo, civet cats, rats, birds, fish, snakes, and such domesticated animals as dogs, chickens, and goats. They occasionally eat crabs, birds, cobras, snails, clams, and even porcupines and macaque monkeys on Flores.

Both core areas and foraging ranges are less rigidly defined than those of other lizard species, probably because the territories are much larger and harder to defend. Several other adult males' foraging ranges overlap with this dragon's, and transient adults and sub-adults will enter his foraging range from time to time, though they try to avoid his core area. By paying careful attention to droppings and scents on the wind, however, he may be able to stay out of eyesight of other hunting dragons and avoid confrontations. Decaying flesh releases putrid oils which are much stronger than the scent of live game, especially by the second day, and any dragon will follow carrion scent as far as 7 miles (11 km) into another's foraging range or even into itscore area. Despite his precautions to avoid any dragon larger than himself, this dragon may well meet several other dangerous dragons — both male and female — over the carcass of a dead deer or boar today.

Young Blood

Spread the jungle crow's wings and fly off to the eastern slopes of the island's tallest mountain, Gunung Ara, which soars 2,412 feet (738 m) above sea level and has already been warmed by the sun. The *tanah dingan* (cool ground) above the 2300-foot (703 m) level is filled with groves of bamboo and rattan, mossy stones, and *Ficus* trees, a pleasant environment for a human trying to escape the sweltering heat, but too cool for any Komodo dragon. Further down are the vast steppes on the mountainside, where 1-foot-tall (30.5 cm), dry *Garnotia* grasses whisper unshaded by any tree. Although deer graze in these high open meadows, there is no shelter from the sun, so few dragons will be found here. Below the 1500-foot (459 m) level, though, the *tanah panas* (hot ground) offers a wealth of micro-climates for the dragons to choose among. Open beach and open savanna are the hottest, since sunlight intensifies when reflecting off the ocean and the hillsides are dotted with lontar palms offering little shade.

Because of the early hour of the day, the soaring jungle crow sees a few 3 foot (.9 m) long specimens hunting rats in the savanna, but they would leave no carrion for a crow, so it circles in closer to the dragons' favorite ranges: lower hillsides and valleys, preferably forested.

A white cockatoo flashes from a clump of dead tamarind trees in the valley floor of a tropical savanna forest, a good site to search for younger dragons. The open canopy allows sunlight to filter through to the lowest levels, especially since the leaves have fallen during the long dry season. The sharp-eyed crow catches sight of movement: a 20 inch (50.8 cm) near-hatchling skillfully climbing the vertical trunk of a tamarind tree. Some reptile species such as crocodiles take close care of their young, both in the eggs and as hatchlings, but Komodo monitors are not among them: half of this young dragon's clutchmates disappeared down an adult dragon's throat while they were still in their eggs. Dragons can hatch at any length from 8-to-19-inches (20.3-to-48.3-cm), but all of them grow quickly, abandoning their clutchmates in less than a month.

Since it hatched in April or May, near the end of the rainy season, this youngster and the others of its generation have already adjusted to their dry season diet of geckoes, skinks, and other lizards. The next rainy season will begin in January, bringing a variety of grass-hoppers and other insects into their diet, and by next dry season, they will be large enough to hunt rats, mice, and birds. At first glance, this two-month-old lizard, already longer than the adults of most other lizard species, looks like a member of some brighter-colored monitor species. Like the first captive-hatched dragons, as described by de Jong (1944), its yellow-green head, neck and forelegs are marked with black stripes and bands; even rows of brick-red circles are arranged in belts along the length of its slim, dark brown body; and its dark brown tail is banded in dull yellow. The protective coloration helps hide it against the sun and shade pattern of the tree trunk. This dragon has spent two days in the tamarind tree, carefully going over its surface and checking under the frequently peeling bark for geckoes and skinks. It now comes down to the ground cautiously, before quickly dashing across the ground to another tree.

> On the basis of present evidence, it seems likely that the greatest predation pressure on oras at all stages of their life is generated from within their own species. ... When competition for food is severe, the eating of young by adult oras is an efficient system of post-hatching recruitment control (Auffenberg, 1981).

In one area studied by Dr. Auffenberg, fecal pellets revealed that other dragons constituted 8.8 percent of the individual animals eaten by larger dragons. From now on until it is a large adult, this dragon will be a solitary animal at constant risk from other members of its own species. Until it reaches about 30 inches (75 cm), it will almost always search for geckoes and insects on or near a tree, stump or log where it can scurry under loose bark or into the hollow of a dead tree when a larger dragon approaches. By the age of nine months through a year and a half, when it is 15 to 40 inches long (40 to 100 cm), it will be dining on rodents and birds, for which it will have to cautiously search on the ground or in burrows, as well as in trees. Other predators the young dragon must be wary of until it reaches 3 feet (about 1 m) in length are feral dogs, boar, brahminy kites (predator-scavenger birds), and snakes.

This youngster is in no risk of being captured by

Indonesian zoo collectors, since they currently gather dragons only on Flores, but as the dragon grows larger and ranges farther, it may have to be wary of occasional poachers who sneak past the rangers' guard. After its first year, the dragon will be too large to jump from branch to branch, but will have to climb slowly and clumsily, using its tail as a prop and occasionally breaking a branch or even falling when it misjudges its new weight. Even as it grows larger, up to 5 feet (1.5 m), it will occasionally shelter in hollow trees, climbing as high as 50 feet (15 m) to find an opening, but it will usually stay about 10 to 13 feet (3 to 4 m) from the ground — out of the adults' way but low enough to see what's going on.

Apparently dragons start scavenging when they are approximately one year old and about 3 feet, 6 inches (1.1 m) in length. Like some species of felines, hyenas, jackals, and raptorial birds, they apparently prefer to scavenge if they have a choice, but are fully capable of killing live game as well. Only a few carrion-eating birds (crows and kites)and some feral dogs are their competitors for carrion on these isolated Indonesian islands. Perhaps this dragon will grow up to be one of the several dozen dragons that gather in the Loho Liang feeding arena to eat the bait goat hung there each weekend, but more likely — if it survives to adulthood — it will join the several thousand other dragons still living wild on the island.

Predator at Work

On the other side of the ridge, a 9-foot-long (2.7 m) dragon is leaving a sunny basking spot and heading down the forested valley. The monsoon trees here bear fruits and nuts eaten by dragons' prey animals, providing a cooler environment since their thick, high canopies allow little sunlight to enter. Most dragons, especially the younger ones, roam over the island with no fixed territory, passing through the activity ranges of several other dragons over the course of several weeks or months. Residents are mostly large males and a few large females. Transients come in all sizes, including large males like this one. Like most adult dragons, this transient finds sentinel, basking, and resting sites uphill, but must move downhill to find deeper shade, food, and water. Although he occasionally crosses a ridge and looks around for prey and other dragons, as a rule he follows smells rather than relying on his sight. This experienced giant usually follows dry creek beds and long savanna valley paths, game trails, and human-created paths. Some trails are so frequently used that they become "virtual ora highways" (Auffenberg, 1981).

There are a number of other dragons in this valley, but the dragon is not searching for any of his kind. Aggression between monitors of the same species, especially Komodo dragons, is so great that chance meetings can lead to severe injury or death. Due to his great size, this dragon is in far less danger than the hatchling, but the ingrained habits of a lifetime keep him from deliberately joining other dragons except at a carrion feast. He bears long, slashing scars from fights in the past, as well as a few puncture scars from attacks on wild boar. The crow settles on a nearby murraya bush, low enough to watch the dragon approach.

Komodo dragons move like other lizards, lifting the front right and rear left feet at the same time, then switching to the opposite feet for the next step. However, other lizard species usually carry their bodies closer to the ground and spend much of their movement time running. The adult dragon stands and walks with knees jutting sideways and front legs akimbo, carrying his body high above the ground and his tail straight out for the first foot, so he looks like he is resting his body and the stem of his tail on a gigantic board. Only the tip of the dragon's tail touches the ground, leaving a track that mirrors the undulations of his walk. Like all adults of his species, this dragon has a long head and neck and a heavy tail almost as long as his body, so his deliberate pace is in "three-part harmony," with the head and tail swinging in one direction and the body in the other with each step.

Why the dragon evolved a bright yellow tongue — it was the only lizard species to do so — is unknown, but the reason that all monitors have forked tongues has been determined. The dragon uses its tongue to "taste" smells, gathering minute particles from the air and ground and putting them against its Jacobson's organs, a sort of paired "super nose" in the roof of its mouth that acts like a combination of taste and smell. Like snakes, which also have Jacobson's organs, monitors use their forked tongues to determine the direction of scents. The human equivalent is not in taste but in hearing; if the same sound reaches both ears but sounds louder in the left ear, the human with normal hearing can assume that the sound came from the left side. The tongue tips are not far enough apart to make this directional reading work well, so the dragon swings its head from side to side as it senses the location of its prey.

The crow moves to an azyma bush to watch the dragon patrolling the edge of the forest, scanning the hot savanna occasionally in search of prey. Each front paw drags forward bent at the wrist so that the top rubs across the ground until the paw is lifted and flopped into place. This inelegant movement is no hardship on feet sturdy as a bear's, though with slightly longer toes; the dragons' sharp-clawed foot is as solid as "the bottom of a brass table leg" (Adams and Carwardine, 1990). Despite his impressive size, this dragon's muscular midsection is relatively lean, indicating that he probably has not eaten a large meal for a week or more. Dragons can and often do die of starvation during the long dry season, and since this dragon is a transient, with no established core area of his own, he may well lead a marginal existence from season to season. Dr. Auffenberg once found an adult dragon "so emaciated it could hardly walk". But this dragon, though no doubt hungry, can survive without food for another three to five weeks if necessary.

A large Russell's viper, disturbed by the vibrations caused by the dragon's heavy steps, slithers across the path toward its hole, but the dragon quickly seizes it behind the head and breaks its back with a strong jerk of his head. Holding the still-twitching body to the ground with one paw, the dragon rips the poisonous snake in two and quickly swallows both halves. Seen in action like this, the thickly muscled legs of this full-sized adult are unlizardly, like a gazelle with the muscular legs of a lion, but the dragon uses his strong legs and sharp-clawed paws not only for lifting and carrying his own large body, but also to dig burrows, excavate megapode bird mounds, climb trees when younger, and scratch females in courtship when older. The well-muscled chest and shoulders play a big part in eating when an adult dragon braces itself and jerks backward to tear chunks off its prey.

By now the still-hungry dragon has entered his ambush spot just outside the shade of the forest, near a path wandering through the tall savanna grasses, which are 1 foot, 6 inches to 13 feet (.5 to 4 meters) high and frequently subject to fire. He clears a space for himself by trampling the grass, then lies flat on the ground, head low and stretched forward in front of him; at this height, he is hidden from any animal coming along the game trail and can get within a yard or so (ca.1 m.) of the intended meal before breaking into a dashing attack. A boar or feral dog might wander by or — if he were on Rinca — a wild horse or monkey, but the dragon is aware that this path through the savanna is most often used by deer.

He might wait several hours for potential prey, but this morning he is lucky and a pregnant doe soon comes cautiously down the path with the rest of her small herd some distance behind her. If she were out in the open, on a beach or where human-set fires have burned clear the grass and reduced the trees, then she could see the dragon and keep a comfortable distance from it. Although dragons can run swiftly, up to 11.5 miles (18.5 km) per hour in a sprint, they do not chase their prey more than a yard or so. When they run, dragons hold their bodies and tails fairly rigid, while the hind feet are swung out wide, giving "the appearance of the movement of a double-ended kayak paddler... [and making a sound] like that of a muffled machine gun," according to Dr.Auffenberg (1981).

The wary doe hears the dragon's approach seconds before he lunges upward at her throat, saliva gleaming on his wide-spread jaws. The doe barely has time to spin around and dash away, her flank marked by a long bloody gash where the dragon slashed her without catching hold. She runs back up the mountain-side, apparently safe, but since the dragons' saliva is highly septic, the wound will probably never heal and she will die from the infection. The eventual eater may or may not be the animal that caused the deer's death but from the standpoint of the Komodo monitor population as a whole, the attack will eventually prove a success. Also, the weakened doe will continue to be a tempting target to dragons, because they may be able to attack while she's in labor or to kill the newborn fawn.

It's difficult to imagine how the Komodo monitor is so successful if one isn't aware of the virulent bacteria in its saliva. The [bacterial] flora includes at least four types that can eventually cause serious blood poisoning in the animal that has been bitten. The resulting infection incapacitates or causes death. If an attack occurred at ten in the morning, the prey could be dead by the end of the day. However, more likely it will take several days. ("Text: Komodo National Park", written text for a Cincinnati Zoo slide presentation)

The unsuccessful dragon moves on to one of the few water holes on Komodo Island that last all year long, a boar wallow. If he were on Rinca or Flores, he might know of a similar water hole created by wild water buffalo. Usually an efficient predator, the dragon has been so active in the blazing sun that he has nearly reached CTM, the critical thermal maximum temperature of 107° to 108° Fahrenheit (41.7° to 42.3° Celsius) that is the most a dragon can tolerate. (Auffenberg, 1988)

He inflates his throat pouch and stretches his mouth wide, panting almost like a dog to expel some of his body heat. The boar still come here, so it is a good place to wait for prey, but right now the dragon drinks deeply from the muddy water hole, plunging his face into the water and scooping a mouthful, then raising his head to let the water roll down his throat. Dragons have also been seen to slurp up water with their tongues, but this one is in a hurry to cool his body down. He continues to thermoregulate by moving into the shade of the monsoon forest that lines the lower section of the valley. Had the dragon killed and eaten the deer, he would have been even more cautious not to get too hot; the raw meat might have rotted in his stomach in the Indonesian heat before it was digested. Regurgitation or even death could result.

Female of the Species

The crow sees a 6-foot-long (1.8 m) dragon sitting

near the path between the visitors' compound and the feeding arena, raised on her forelegs with her nine-vertebrae neck stretched improbably high to look above the surface of the grass. An adult dragon can lie so close to the ground that it will be hidden in 8-inch-tall (20 cm) grass, but its long neck allows it to stretch high enough to see above 15-inch-tall (40 cm) grass. This lizard still occasionally sits up tripod-like, balancing on its back legs and tail to see above the tall grasses, a habit she learned when, as a youngster, she used her tail as a prop as she climbed trees. No longer slender, light weight, and nimble, she has grown clumsier and considerably bulkier in recent years and can no longer climb a tree success-fully. On the other hand, her strong legs and thick shoulders and neck make her a much more effective hunter of large animals and improve her skill at tearing apart the large bodies of prey.

Dragons habitually use the forest paths beaten through the underbrush by prey animals and humans, just like they appropriate natural holes in the ground and claim those dug by other animals. The feeding arena is in a valley, in the savanna-monsoon forest region where dragons are most comfortable. Should a human come along this path, she may choose to retreat, but it will be with her tail lifted and curved sideways, ready to slap if the person attacks. For fighting or reaching food sus-pended as bait, even very large dragons can raise them-selves on their hind legs, with their tails serving to balance them, like the third leg of a tripod. This dragon is among the closest tourists will find to a tame dragon, since she comes regularly to the feeding arena whenever she sees humans coming down the path. When no people ap-proach, however, she knows no food will be provided today and turns away.

Dragon skin has been described as looking like chain mail: on an adult dragon, the drapes of thick skin are particularly obvious at the throat, elbows, knees, and in a long "pleat" down the length of each side. Up close, the osteoderms ("skin bones"), pebble-like bumps which pepper the dragon's skin, are clearly the reason why dragon skin has never been commercially used as leather for shoes or purses.

Most dragons reach sexual maturity at five to seven years, and a female this large may be considered a mature adult, though her age is difficult to guess. Although she does not fit the human image of feminine, this dragon's gender is proven by the oldest scientific test when she moves off the path to a gently sloping hillside with few rocks. She mated about two weeks ago, and the burrow she is now digging is an indication that she is about to begin laying eggs. Although the Ragunan Zoo in Jakarta has filmed a female dragon simply laying her eggs in a depression on the ground, this dragon is taking the time to dig a U-shaped burrow and lay her eggs in the bottom of it. With a shivering head, she lifts her tail at the base, her rear legs raising her groin slightly above the ground as two eggs drop from her body. It may be an hour before she lays another pair, or she may continue to lay eggs sporadically over the next several weeks. This is the only clutch she will lay this year, and the number of eggs may range from one to 30. The eggs, which have a soft, smooth, leathery shell, measure between 2 1/3 to 4 1/2 inches (5.9 to 11.4 cm) in length.

Since there are so many more male dragons than females, the chances of each mature female dragon bearing eggs each year is quite high. Auffenberg (1981) estimated the annual hatchling crop on Komodo to be 1,500 dragons based on the following formula: "400 mature females x 15 eggs/average nest = 25 percent nesting success." By laying her clutch in this burrow, the dragon may increase the eggs' chances of being successfully hatched, but of course many dangers await the infant dragons in the years to come.

Scavenger

On another valley forest trail, a subadult dragon is found, prowling cautiously down a forest path, her head swinging low from side to side and her yellow forked tongue flickering from between her closed lips to taste the air and ground. The 4 foot, 6 inches long dragon has sensed carrion nearby, but within the home range of a much larger male. To a human, the smell of the two-days-dead animal would be overripe and foul, but dragons find this almost an ideal meal: another several days, and the carcass might decompose, be mummified from the hot sun or be eaten by scarabid beetles that can finish off a goat carcass in 48 hours. The dead water buffalo should provide plenty of food for both the larger and smaller lizard, and, even, other dragons who, smelling the dead animal, will soon invade the larger male's range as well. A festering gash on the rear leg of the carcass shows the cause of death; at some point it was attacked by a dragon and the infected wound never healed.

Subadult dragons usually walk with the stiff, formal gait of young crocodiles. This dragon is just on the point of maturity and is willing to risk taking part in a feeding aggregation. The newcomer steps forward cautiously, holding her body high and slightly arched, head forward and a little down, in an appeasement gesture toward the larger male. Dr. Auffenberg (1978) has identified this visual communication as a defensive tactic, which can quickly switch to a threat display.

The larger dragon pays no apparent attention, for he is absorbed in tearing open the stomach of the fallen animal. With braced legs, he rips a large chunk of intestines free, shakes his head violently so that the contents of the stomach go flying, then gulps most of the intestines down in a single swallow. Another dragon, almost as large as the first, hurries into the glen, darting forward when the first dragon's head is buried in the buffalo's flank. The startled dragon jumps back and both large adults hiss at each other, inflating the pouches in their throats and stretching their mouths wide open. They arch their bodies sideways and curl their tails back, each ready to strike. To a human observer, they would seem to be glaring at each other, since part of the threat behavior is to tilt the head sideways and look at the opponent from under the heavy brow ridge.

The smaller dragon sees her chance and darts forward to grab the carcass by its haunch. Another, medium-sized dragon enters the scene, and the larger dragons abandon their stand-off. Already two feral dogs have gathered several yards away and are barking at the dragons, hoping to scare them away and eat the carrion themselves. The larger dragons ignore the dogs, and, though the smaller dragons are nervous about their presence, the dogs dare not come closer with so many dragons present. Every dragon now tries simply to swallow as much food as possible before the next dragon eats it, though the two larger dragons get the best parts and the most food. With tearing movements, they separate large pieces of flesh and bone from the carcass and quickly swallow without chewing. Since the carcass is in the shade, the dragons can feed without fear of overheating, and most if not all of the body should be gone in a few hours. Dr. Auffenberg once observed a dragon over 8 feet (2.5 m) long swallow a 33 pound (15 kg) hog after it had been eviscerated. Another dragon was seen swallowing a month-old fawn without tearing out the gut first, and a dragon weighing about 110 pounds (50 kgs) ate a 90 pound (40 kg) wild hog in 17 minutes. Even individual dragons may consume a large animal at a single feeding and then not eat again for several days or up to a week.

The dragons salivate a great deal while eating, probably to lubricate the huge sections that they often swallow whole, but when their saliva turns bloody, it is often because the spongy skin of their own gums is being cut against the sharp edges of their teeth as they bite and tear the meat. The dragons eat very rapidly and without discrimination, benefiting from the sharp, curved teeth ideal for grasping and cutting, and the specialized joints which allow their jaws to stretch amazingly wide so they can swallow huge chunks of meat. Even their broad flat jaws give them a wider feeding capacity than other monitors of similar size, and teeth lost in the violence of eating or fighting are quickly replaced.   The dragons sneeze frequently as they eat, dislodging fly larvae from their nasal passages. Considering the fact that they prefer carrion over live prey, dragons in the wild may expect to often encounter flies and even maggots in their food.

Mating Rituals

Dragon courtship frequently occurs when male and female dragons encounter each other while feeding on carrion or a fresh kill. Courtship can take place any time between January and October, but most actual mating takes place during July and August. Although it is the right time of year for breeding, the small female at this feeding aggregation is too young to mate.   When the dragons finish eating, some wipe their jaws in the grass, but the young dragon runs off with a length of intestine still dangling from her mouth. The medium-sized dragon quarrels with two crows over dollops of meat left in the grass until a feral dog scares them all away. Now only a hoof and the horns are left. The two larger dragons are so full that their stomachs sag to the ground, yet if they were of opposite sexes, this would be the ideal time for mating.
A dragon rendezvous is more like bumping carts

in a crowded supermarket than taking a date to a restaurant, since any dragon that smells fresh blood or carrion will invite itself to the feast and the larger adults may quarrel fiercely over pieces of meat. Lizard anatomy makes it impossible for the male to mount the female from behind as most animals do, as the tail gets in the way. All lizard and snake species have evolved an alternative reproductive system to allow the males to approach the females from the side. In lizards, this posture is roughly similar to the position assumed by a pair of wrestlers at the start of a match. Each male is equipped with hemipenes, which in the normal state are retracted within the tail and cannot be seen simply by turning the snake or lizard over. Only one hemipenis is used in mating; if the male mounts on the female's left side, his right hemipenis is in position for insertion.

"[M]ales interested in mating must be able to so completely restrain the females that they remain uninjured after breeding," Auffenberg (1981) stated, noting that during courtship the female dragons are apt to engage in combative displays and use their teeth and tails more than the males. Large male dragons may also include an element of hostility in their courtship, particularly since it takes place in a competitive feeding situation. However, the male usually courts his potential mate more gently, by tonguing and then rubbing his chin on the sides and top of her body and neck. The female may show her interest by tonguing the male in return, or she may respond aggressively or run away, with the male following close behind. Before mounting the female, the male always rakes her back with his sharp claws to persuade her to lie still — he may also bite her neck. After some courtship behavior, the male dragon will mount the female from the side. He may bite or scratch her about the neck and shoulders, possibly to ensure that she does not struggle. Although lizard breeding is brief and without much thrusting, the hard scales of the adult dragons can make it a noisy process.

An Afternoon's Work

With all the prey eaten, the crow flies away as well, heading toward Gunung Klinta, the mountain on the eastern side of Telok Slawi (Python Bay). Fifteen hundred feet (450 m) of roaring waters pour through the dangerous strait between Komodo and Nusa Mbarapu, a tiny island out in the bay, now dotted with grey and white shapes. Some villagers from Komodo have carried their goats across the sea to pasture on this small land mass only 1/5 of a square mile (.6 square m). From this high view, the crow watches a natural drama unfold below. On the Komodo beach below, a large dragon launches itself into the waves, quickly diving below the choppy surface to the calmer waters below. But the strait is seldom calm, since it is torn by a strong tidal current and many whirlpools. After swimming about 300 feet (100 m), the dragon rises to the surface for air. While underwater, the dragon is about 20 feet (6 m) below the surface, swimming with its legs tucked in against its body and the powerful tail swinging side to side to propel it through the water. The dragon continues its determined path through the ocean, arriving at last in a place where no humans and no other predators will disturb its predation.

Although the trip seemed daring and difficult, the dragon was unable to resist such a good source of potential prey. Perhaps it has swum this gap before, for the villagers have lost goats on Nusa Mbarapu to visiting dragons in the past. Fishermen spreading their catch on the beach have sometimes had to gather it up hurriedly when a dragon stepped out of the roaring surf. Adult dragons can cross this strait at will, but, since the only prey on Nusa Mbarapu is that unwillingly supplied by

humans, dragons cannot permanently settle on the island, and this dragon will return when it has finished
feasting or is driven away by humans.

Another example of dragons' swimming skill
was demonstrated in a story told to Dick and Mary Lutz
on Rinca. After a dragon killed a child on Rinca in 1986,
government rangers transported the dragon to another
island to prevent the villagers from killing it in revenge.
Upon its release, the dragon simply swam back to Rinca
Island.

Dr. Auffenberg's study revealed that deer, boar,
and monkeys are available as prey on the 3.8-square-mile
(10-square-km) island of Oewada Sami and the four-
square-mile (10.2-square-km) island of Gili Mota features
deer and boar; dragons have been seen on both islands
and Dr. Auffenberg believes some live permanently on
both islands (Auffenberg, 1981).

As the crow flies back over Komodo, vast sections
of the island fall into shadow where the sun has dropped
below the mountain peaks. A few dragons here and there
are searching for one last meal before the day's end.
Beside one forest path, a patient dragon digs into the
massive incubating mound of a megapode bird nest in
search of eggs, while a smaller specimen climbs a tamarind tree trunk toward a green jungle fowl giving its
evening crow. Night falls around 6:30 p.m., but during
the long dry season there are many bright moonlit nights.
Although the temperature is refreshingly cool after the
blazing heat of the summer day, dragons do not roam at
night, except for those who were far from their burrows
when the sun set. In fact, because so few dragons are
residents, the various burrows seen in the daytime may
be inhabited in the evening by different transient dragons
from night to night; rather like humans' hotel rooms, not
all are filled nightly, and transients do not necessarily
return to the same hole each time they wander into a
region.

By 7:30 p.m., Dr. Auffenberg (1981)and his assis-
tants found they could manipulate sleeping dragons to
attach marker tags and take tick samples without even
waking them. Only occasionally would they come across
a dragon still awake but motionless in its burrow as late
as 11:30 p.m. The final image the weary crow carries
away at evening's end is best described in Dr. Auffenberg's
words:

> [T]hey would lie in the grass or in their holes, with
> head outside the mouth of the burrow and eyes
> wide open, staring into the black surrounding
> forest (Auffenberg, 1981).

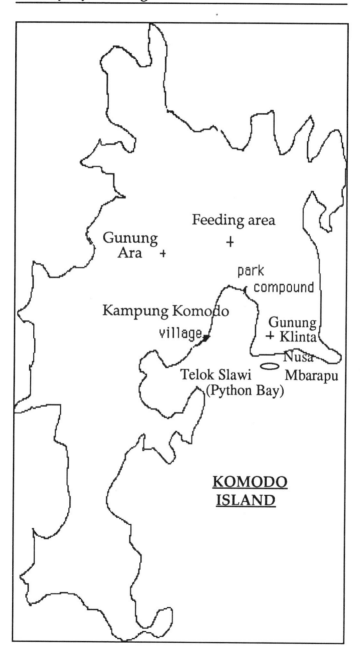

Feeding area
+

Gunung
Ara +

park
compound

Kampung Komodo
village

Gunung
+ Klinta

Nusa
Telok Slawi   Mbarapu
(Python Bay)

KOMODO
ISLAND

4

ORIGIN OF THE SPECIES

Set the controls of an imaginary time machine to the year of the American Revolution — 1776 — but instead of investigating the British Empire's war with its unruly New World colonies, peek over the shoulder of a German fossil collector exploring in Belgium. For centuries, humans digging deep into the earth for mines or wells have found fossils, but the massive reptile skull coming to light under Dr. Hoffman's cleaning brush is an unprecedented find: the remains of an extinct species. Although at first believed to be the skull of a whale or crocodile, *Mosasaurus hoffmanni* will later prove by the shape of its jaws and skull to be an ancient sea-dwelling ancestor of the monitor lizards, perhaps reaching 33 feet (10 m) in length.

The time machine rockets through the next century and a half, touching on highlights in the development of paleontology. Fossils continue to be uncovered throughout the world, and by 1830, scientists have discovered five major groups of extinct reptiles, including dinosaurs. In 1859, Charles Darwin publishes *On the Origin of Species by Means of Natural Selection* based on his discoveries in the Galapagos Islands, an immediate bestseller which explains how species evolve through survival of the fittest. Alfred Russel Wallace, who arrived at the same theory after visiting the Dutch East Indies, misses his chance in the history books by not publishing first. Beginning in 1880, fossil-hunting expeditions start digs throughout the western American frontier from Montana to Colorado. The exaggerated account of one of these expeditions is blazoned across a New York paper as the time machine comes to rest, invisible, behind a millionaire reading the news at his breakfast table.

Andrew Carnegie has already made his fortune and established the Carnegie Institute in Pittsburgh, Pennsylvania before that fateful morning in 1898. By the time he rises from the table and folds the paper, the influential millionaire has caught dinosaur fever and will soon infect the nation with this "disease." Over the next decade, hundreds of dinosaur bones are found in one spectacularly successful dig after another in both Wyoming and Utah; Carnegie's Midas touch affected the expeditions he sponsored. A dinosaur hall is added to the Carnegie Institute, and pride of place is given to the 84-foot-long (25.2 m) *Diplodocus* skeleton discovered in 1904. Full-sized casts of the huge artifact are made and presented to the leaders of seven European nations to put in their national museums, and, as a result, a popular tavern song echoes across the United States and Europe:

> Crowned heads of Europe
> All make a royal fuss
> Over Uncle Andy
> And his old *Diplodocus* (Krishtalka, 1989).

Due to "Uncle Andy's" *Diplodocus* and other massive dinosaur fossils, which dwarf and overwhelm the fossils of other extinct species, the popular belief arose that all extinct ancient reptiles were dinosaurs. Today's expert seven-year-old, correctly identifying plastic toys of ichthyosaurs, pleisosaurs, and pterodactyls, will insist that they represent dinosaurs — as will the adult who taught her. However, dinosaurs were only one late and relatively small superorder of the class that dominated the Age of Reptiles.

Taxonomy, the organizational method that defines the genetic and ancestral relationships between different types of living beings helps to explain dinosaurs' small role in the reptile class. The animal kingdom is divided into two phyla: animals with backbones and those without (sea anemones and worms, for example). Within Chordata (the animals with backbones) are the basic classes of birds, reptiles, amphibians, fish, and mammals. Taxonomy at its most basic level provides the following family tree for the *Diplodocus* found in 1899.

> Class: Reptilia
> Order: Saurischia
> Genus: *Diplodocus*

To clarify the ancestry of living and extinct reptiles, more levels can be added to taxonomic categories, divisions such as subclasses and superorders. The complete taxonomy of Komodo dragons is shown below.

Class: Reptilia
  Subclass: Diapsida
    Superorder: Lepidosauria
      Order: Squamata
        Suborder: Sauria
          Infraorder: Anguimorpha
            Superfamily: Platynota
              Family: Varanidae
                Genus: *Varanus*
                  Species: *V. komodoensis*

Instead of reciting an animal's complete taxonomy whenever it is discussed, scientists identify animals primarily by genus (like *Diplodocus*) or by genus and species (like *Homo sapiens*).

Relicts of the Dinosaur Age?

Two hundred and sixty million years ago, the Age of Amphibians climaxed with *Eryops*, a 6-foot-long (1.8 m) "crocodile-hippopotamus" that lived on the edges of lakes and rivers, eating land animals as well as fish (Colbert, 1955). How could the newly-evolved reptiles compete with this specimen? Charles Darwin and Alfred Russel Wallace would be the first to point out the reptiles' advantage: by evolving shell-protected eggs, they vastly expanded their ability to live and reproduce on dry land. Over millions of years, amphibians, limited by the need to lay their eggs in water, dwindled in size and importance.

The Age of Reptiles spanned the Mesozoic era, lasting approximately 145,000,000 years. Nature evolved variation upon variation of reptilian orders, many of which survived for millions of years and parented new orders before dying out completely.

For example, Anapsida, the first subclass from which all other reptiles evolved, produced two orders which became extinct and the only offspring order to survive unchanged is Chelonia, the turtles. As Charles Darwin and Alfred Russel Wallace were later to clarify, all animal and plant species must constantly evolve to match the changing environment, and those which fail to do so eventually become extinct.

The most important reptilian subclass from the human perspective was Synapsida, which evolved into the first mammals approximately 220,000,000 years ago, about the same time that dinosaurs evolved. The next reptilian subclass, Diapsida, had already evolved the first

of two superorders: Lepidosauria, which included lizards and Rhynchocephalia(the lizard-like beak-headed
reptiles) and would eventually include snakes. Now the
second superorder evolved: Archosauria, which included the pterosaurs and the two orders of dinosaurs
and would later include the crocodilians. Of the dinosaur
orders — Saurischia and Ornithischia — the first would
leave only one living descendant group, the birds, while
the other died out completely. Two entire subclasses of
reptiles — Euryapsida and Parapsida — also disappeared
from the earth by the end of the Mesozoic era; *Ichthyosaurus*
and many other genera within these extinct subclasses
are often mistaken for dinosaurs in popular belief.

"The oldest lizards antedate the earliest dinosaurs by a full thirty million years. A few large lizards,
such as the man-eating Komodo dragon, have been called
'relicts of the dinosaur age', but this phrase is historically
incorrect," Bakker (1986) later explained in *The Dinosaur
Heresies*.

The true relict of the dinosaur age — other than
their only living descendants, the birds — is the tuatara,
a little known reptile that is the only living descendant of
the prehistoric Rhynchocephalia, the beak-heads.

> The order Rhynchocephalia was extremely suc-
> cessful up through the Cretaceous but is un-
> known as fossils in the last 75 million years. A
> single species, the tuatara, survives today. New
> Zealand. It is sometimes called a living fossil,
> although the term is a semantic absurdity (Sav-
> age, 1963).

While the Squamata order produced every snake
and lizard species in existence, as well as many others
now extinct, the beak-heads (named after their turtle-like
mouths), evolved along one narrow line with little
adaptive variation.

The tuatara, a mild, foot-long (ca .3 m) reptile which resembles a chunky, big-headed lizard, shows its ancestry only upon dissection, for its skeletal and anatomical design are more ancient than those of any reptile on the earth today. Rhynchocephalians were not dinosaurs, but they were a living, evolving order in the dinosaur age, and it is a small miracle that the tuatara found a quiet enough backwater to survive in while the world evolved around it.

Herpetologist Peter Strimple, in a 1991 conversation, noted that *Sphenodon punctatus* is not the only species in the *Sphenodon* genus. A variation in tuataras — remarkable in such a small, geographically limited population — is now established as a separate species. The fact that *Sphenodon guntheri* is now established as a valid species is an indication that the tuatara is continuing to evolve.

Some of the best headlines of the early 1900's were about reptiles which had roamed the earth millions of years before, and the Komodo dragon's fearsome appearance and great size led the popular press to label it as a "living dinosaur."

Despite scientists' explanation that some ancestral lizards were much larger than the smallest dinosaurs and the lizard suborder is older than both dinosaur orders, when Douglas Burden returned from his famous expedition, the American press plagued him with questions about dinosaurs.

> I have been asked repeatedly if it is true that these beasts are prehistoric — that favorite epithet of the newspapers, and, for the reason that the term is rather meaningless, I confess to finding the question difficult to answer. In the literal sense, every living organism is prehistoric, for are not we all, man included,

the outcome of millions of years of evolution? If, however, the word has come to mean great age with little change, it is correctly applied to these carnivorous lizards of Komodo. For the truth is they are the oldest of living lizards, dating back to early Eocene time [40 million to 60 million years ago], the beginning of the age of mammals (Burden, 1927).

Ancestral Dragons

More recent scientific evidence indicates that Burden's estimate places the Komodo dragons too late in time, but the ancestry of monitor lizards may be traced at least as far back as the Cretaceous era of 70,000,000 to 135,000,000 years ago. Before ancestral monitors evolved, dinosaurs grew to dominate earth during the Jurassic era (135,000,000 to 180,000,000 years ago), so other reptiles as well as mammals decreased in size or developed other ways of avoiding the monstrous "thunder-lizards." The early sauria that were to become the monitors' ancestors took the highly unusual technique of evolving into marine reptiles, first 3-to-6-foot-long (1-to-2--m) aigialosaurs and dolichosaurs that were equally comfortable on land or in the water, and then the huge mosasaurs that lived entirely in the ocean unless they laid their eggs on beaches like the giant sea turtles do today (Bellairs, Life: I, 1970).

Members of the Dolichosauridae family had as many as 17 vertebrae in their necks and the Aigialosauridae had up to 12 or 13, an indication of their relationship to monitors, which have nine vertebrae, while all other lizards have eight or fewer (Williston, 1914). By comparison, humans and giraffes and most other mammals have a mere seven vertebrae. The taxonomy of the mosasaur species discovered by Dr. Hoffman is given below.

Subclass: *Diapsida*
  Superorder: *Lepidosauria* (pleasant-lizards)
    Order: *Squamata* (scaly)
      Suborder: *Sauria* (lizards)
        Infraorder: *Anguimorpha* (snake-like)
          Superfamily: *Platynota*
            Family: *Mosasauridae*
              Genus: *Mosasaurus*
                Species:*hoffmanni*

The *Mosasauridae* had crocodile-like bodies and flippers instead of legs; with their 30-foot (9 m) length, long jaws and sharp, pointed teeth, they were the top predator in the ocean hierarchy. The mosasaurs also had double-hinged jaws, not just the joint where the jaw attaches to the skull, but another hinge behind the teeth which enabled the sea-lizards to swallow whole fish 6 or 7 feet long (1.8 or 2.1 m) (Williston, 1914).

A trace of this double-hinged jaw remains in the monitors alone, of all modern lizards, and helps explain why Komodo dragons attack such large quadrupeds as horses and water buffalo. Mosasaurs became extinct around the time that dinosaurs died out, but their descendants re-developed legs and returned to land, gradually evolving into the *Varanidae* (varanids are the monitor family).

It seems probable that the ancient varanids began their life on land in what is now Eurasia. The earliest genus of the *Varanidae* family — what one might call the Komodo dragon's first direct ancestor — appeared approximately 70,000,000 to 100,000,000 years ago (Carroll, 1988). In fact, John Horner and James Gorman (1988) note that varanid remains have been found in a nest with dinosaur eggs from the same date. This overlap between the dwindling dinosaurs and the emerging varanids occurred in the Late Cretaceous, just as dinosaurs were dying out and the Age of Mammals was beginning. Fossil varanids from the Late Cretaceous, Paleocene, and Eocene eras have been found in North America, Europe and Mongolia, indicating that members of the family migrated to all areas of what was then one connected land mass in the northern hemisphere. The shifting of continents and the rise and fall of land masses played a great role in monitors' ancestry.

For example, many animal species crossed the land bridge then existing between Siberia and Alaska;varanid immigrants to the New World may even have encountered and fed on early zebras going the other way. But the colonies of varanids died out in what is now the North American continent, and no modern lizard species would attempt to cross what is now a frozen island-dotted sea between two continents. The vast southern land mass of Gondwanaland was home to other lizard families but not to varanids; when a portion of what is now Antartica broke off to become the South American continent, the large teiid lizards, such as the muscular 4-foot-long (1.2 m) tegu, grew to occupy the environmental niche that monitors now claim in Asia. (Hecht, 1975)

Each reptile class found a method of surviving in the same environment with the more efficient and active warm-blooded animals that evolved to rule the earth in the Age of Mammals. Turtles evolved shells; snakes became skilled at burrowing and hiding, and many developed poisonous defenses; crocodilians moved to tropical environments where they were often the primary predators; and tuataras retreated to a region of New Zealand unpopulated by mammals (Colbert, 1955).

For the most part, lizards adjusted by developing protective colorations and camouflage to match their environments. The bolder, larger varanids were a notable exception, as shown by*Megalania prisca,* the giant land lizard of Pleistocene Australia. Discovered by noted English paleontologist Sir Richard Owen in 1860, *Megalania prisca* is now known to have been the largest terrestrial lizard, growing to 20 to 23 feet (6 or 7 m) in length. Sir Owen, the man who invented the term "dinosaur," was also the discoverer of one of the monitors' more ancient ancestors, the dolichosaurs. Modern scholars feel certain they have identified *Megalania* as the closest relative, living or extinct, of the modern monitor lizards, especially the Komodo dragon. Its taxonomy shows the close relationship between the two genera.

Subclass: *Diapsida*
   Superorder: *Lepidosauria*
      Order: *Squamata*
         Suborder: *Sauria*
            Infraorder: *Anguimorpha*
               Superfamily: *Platynota*
                  Family: *Varanidae*
                     Genus: *Megalania*
                        Species: *M. prisca*

Since Australia, like South America and Africa, was once a part of the southern hemisphere's prehistoric super-continent of Gondwanaland, paleontologists are forced to believe that *Megalania's* ancestors were colonists from Eurasia, and were a branch of the family which survived while the North American immigrants became extinct. Without a continuous land mass connecting Asia and Australia, the early varanids must have swum across the seas between the early continents.

The dispersal over the enlarged water gap must have been a formidable feat, thus limiting the number of varanid forms which were capable of making the invasion. ... Whereas the *Varanidae* occur in Africa, another Gondwana continent, the invasion must have been very recent as evidenced by the lack of varanid fossils in the Miocene and Pliocene (Hecht, 1975).

Measurements of fossil remains build a picture of *Megalania* as a heavily built monitor lizard with neck and upper arms shorter than usual to help carry the weight of its huge head and body. The teeth are pointed but slightly more curved than those of Komodo dragons, indicating that *Megalania* was also a carnivore which tore its prey apart in huge chunks. Unlike the sinuous, long-tailed iguanas, Komodo dragons generally have tails no longer than their bodies (half of the body length to the whole body length); according to paleontologist Max Hecht (1975), the ancestral monitor's tail may have been even shorter in relation to its body, perhaps one third to one half of the body length. Even taking the relatively short tail into consideration, Dr. Hecht estimated that it is possible to project the maximum length of *Megalania* as nearly 23 feet (7 m), with a weight of about 1,300 pounds (591 kg). Diamond (1987) indicated that later studies estimate a length of 20 feet (6.1 m) and a weight of 4500 pounds (2,045 kg), nearly four times heavier than the 1975 estimate.

The Primary Consumer

Alfred Russel Wallace, the "other Darwin," traveled throughout southeast Asia (primarily what is today known as Indonesia) from 1854 to 1862, gathering specimens of all kinds and recording information about the various peoples and areas he visited. The naturalist noticed the extreme variations in plant and animal life between the eastern and western islands. Borneo, Bali, and the other western islands clearly had close biological ties to the Orient, while Celebes (now Sulawesi), Lombok and the rest of the eastern islands (including Komodo) contained life forms similar to those of Australia. He developed the hypothesis that the flora and fauna of the entire region are divided by what has come to be known as 'Wallace's Line.' This imaginary line, running between Bali and Lombok only some 300 miles (480 km) west of Komodo, marks the division between flora and fauna found elsewhere in Asia and flora and fauna found in Australia. The eastern Indonesian islands, including the Lesser Sunda Islands that are the Komodo dragon's home, are still called Wallacea by zoogeographers.

It was later realized the earth can be divided into six realms — not kingdoms in the human sense, but separate territories with distinct climates and terrains which serve as barriers to species migration (Considine, 1976). For example, the tropical forests that begin in southern Mexico and continue through most of Central and South America are utterly different in temperature and moisture from northern Mexico and the rest of North America. Buffalo, antelopes, and beavers could not survive in South American jungles, nor could such southern natives as monkeys, jaguars, and tree sloths exist in the colder, dryer plains and mountains of North America.

Because the Australian realm was part of Gondwanaland, early mammals evolved quite differently from the mammals of the Oriental realm; Australia developed only marsupial mammals, while Asia, on the other side of Wallace's line, became the home to placental mammals. Instead of deer, gazelles, woodchucks, squirrels, and rabbits, modern Australia has a parallel marsupial population of wallabies, kangaroos, wombats, koalas, and bandicoots. A population of marsupial carnivores consumes these herbivorous prey: the Tasmanian wolf and the Tasmanian devil take the place of wolves or tigers, while smaller marsupial ant-eaters and moles assume the role of   bobcats, cheetahs, and weasels (Colbert, 1955).

Plant-eating animals must spend a great deal of their time grazing in order to obtain enough needed protein, but actual eating occupies relatively little of the meat-eaters' time, since they get a massive jolt of concentrated protein whenever they eat other animals. Predatory carnivores instead devote their lives to capturing their food "on the hoof" while scavengers either follow predators around in search of a meal or find dead animals on their own. Both types of carnivores are in constant competition with other animals for their prey.

"Giant predator lizards can't evolve in the presence of big mammal predators," Bakker (1986) notes, and Hecht (1975) holds the same opinion, stating that when the varanids arrived on Australia, the carnivore niche was almost empty, which "allowed for the opportunistic development of the primary consumer." The dinner table for *Megalania* was full of large herbivores—wombat ancestors as large as oxes, giant kangaroos and rhinoceros-like marsupials, and tasty *Macropodia* (giant turkey-like birds that were ancestors to Komodo Island's megapode birds) — but, because of Wallace's line, the usual major carnivorous predators were missing from the Australian landscape. These megafauna had almost no natural enemies: just one highly specialized marsupial lion and the giant varanid *Megalania*. (Colbert, 1966; Hecht, 1975; Diamond, 1987). Like its ancestor *Mosasaurus*, the "reptile shark" of the sea during the dinosaur age, *Megalania* was the "reptile tiger" of Australia during the Pleistocene.

By the time prehistoric Komodo dragons had evolved, however, conditions were different. The early monitor had dwindled to less than half the size of *Megalania*; indeed, it is entirely possible that it became smaller than today's Komodo dragon. Perhaps the giant herbivores were too large for the prehistoric *Varanus komodoensis* to prey on or the slower and smaller prey may have become extinct. At some point in time, too, the few marsupial predators of modern Australia began to evolve into the large predator niche. Several big monitor species and a number of smaller ones evolved successfully in Australia, but the prehistoric *V.komodoensis* found a better opportunity by taking to water.

The vast distance between Australia and the Lesser Sunda Islands is now known as the Timor Sea, but it was nowhere near as large a gap in the Pleistocene era. The continental shelf offshore of Australia was then above water, and it reached almost as far north as Timor Island, apparently a distance that was within the swimming abilities of the early monitor.

> From Timor, *[V.] komodoensi* s could have made its way, step by step, along the old outer arc of volcanic islands to Sumba... The next jump from Sumba to Komodo under the influence of the same southeasterly trade winds is no more difficult to bridge than the original Timor jump (Burden, 1928).

What did Komodo dragon ancestors find when they climbed up the beaches after their oceanic journeys? The new land must have been paradise, in their eyes. First of all, it really was new, an isolated island mass that, after numerous earthquakes and volcanic eruptions, would become the three separate islands of Komodo, Padar and Rinca. Geological proof of the modern islands' relative youth lies in the recently elevated coral reefs found on the flanks of some islands, indicating that many small islands and portions of larger ones in Wallacea were formed or modified in very late geological time. Dr. Auffenberg (1981) points out that the entire Indonesian region is a zone still subjected to diatrophism —techtonic plate movement deforming the earth's crust — and volcanism. There must have been a succession of land surfaces in the Komodo area since its earliest developmental phases, but the lizard species that swam from Australia to Timor to the Komodo land mass could migrate as necessary to keep up with the geological changes.

Food sources were probably varied, then as now. Birds and their eggs would have been available, including *Macropodia*, the incubator bird that also migrated from Australia. Still a major food source for middle-sized dragons, the birds lay their eggs in immense incubating mounds that the dragons have learned to dig up. David Attenborough (1984) suggests that the dragon ancestors probably ate insects, small mammals, and carrion, the diet for many other modern monitor species.

All other lizards would also have been good prey, which may explain why the common Malayan monitor, *Varanus salvator* , thrives on islands to the east and west of Komodo, but does not live on any of the islands in the dragons' range, except for a slight overlap on Flores. According to Jared Diamond (1987), although it is clear that buffalo, horses, and goats were not introduced until humans arrived in the region about 4000 B.C., the Rusa deer and wild boar may have arrived on their own, escaping the large predators of other islands. There is also some fossil evidence to support Dr. Auffenberg's belief that pygmy elephants, now extinct, must have been plentiful when the monitor species arrived (Auffenberg, 1981).

Best of all, there were no large predator species in the region, and without enemies or competitors, the modern Komodo dragon evolved to fill the ecological niche. No fossil evidence has been uncovered to prove whether the species was already large enough to thrive on the existing large herbivorous mammals, or whether the dragons grew large enough "to tap a rich and otherwise unexploited source of meat" (Attenborough, 1984). In either case, the Komodo dragon had found a paradise where it was to reign unmolested for ten million years. It had found its home.

5

KOMODO DRAGONS IN CAPTIVITY

Komodo dragons are an exotic and little-known species that were originally sought for zoo collections because of their "freak" appeal. The first dragons collected were the two brought live to the Buitenzorg (Bogor) Botanical Garden and Museum in 1912. How long these dragons lived in captivity and how large they grew is not recorded. The size, fierce appearance, carnivorous habits, and man-eating reputation of Komodo dragons fascinated the general public from the first, and therefore made them a favorite with zoo curators. Zoogoers were later pleased to learn of the relative docility of many zoo dragons, beginning with those kept in London and Frankfurt in the 1920's and 1930's.

> When captured, and placed in a cage in the zoo, as a general rule it [the Komodo dragon species] becomes very docile and tame, far tamer than any other reptilian, save some of the giant tortoises. While some individuals remain wary, the majority, regardless of size, become ideal zoo exhibits (Jones, 1964).

In "Twentieth Century Dragons," Mario DePrato of the National Zoo in Washington, D.C., described the increasing tameness of the zoo's dragons, especially a female kept by the zoo for at least seven years. In 1964, Renee and her first mate made the long trip from Indonesia by airplane and then from the Baltimore airport by truck; when her traveling crate was opened she ran out and tried to attack Mario DePrato, chasing him around the cage. After they adjusted to their new home, both dragons became tame toward their keepers, although the male soon died of an amoebic infection. A second male, acquired years later, soon grew accustomed to drinking water from the palm of his keeper's hand. Beginning in 1971, Mario DePrato wrote of Renee following him around the enclosure, crawling over him and licking him for sensory information as she would another dragon. He described the dragons as being "like two puppies"; they both enjoyed warm-water baths and being scrubbed with a soft brush, and would come over to the keeper whenever he entered the enclosure to see if he had any food to offer.

When Komodo dragons were discovered, Major Ouwens and others at first believed them to be deaf, but soon zookeepers began reporting otherwise. Lady Broughton (1936) fired a shotgun near some Komodo dragons in the wild and found they completely ignored the noise, yet she later told of zoo specimens quick to hear the sound of the key turning in the lock of their cage at feeding time. The species are apparently simply uninterested in human-caused sounds which they consider unimportant. Certainly their position as the only large carnivore native to their islands would not train the giant lizards to be fearful of sounds caused by other species.

Since the 1920's, various zookeepers have taught their dragons to come in response to a call or whistle, usually associated with feeding time. Mario DePrato reported on the process of training Renee to react to his whistle.

> During her stay in the outside enclosure, I
> started using various calls, shouts, and
> whistles. I found a sort of two-phase whistle
> which I used constantly. ... At first she showed
> no sign of recognition; then she finally recog-
> nized it and would jerk her head up, if lying
> down, and try to distinguish the direction
> from which the sound was coming.... She, at
> times, would be in the house asleep or in the
> moat out of sight; yet, when I whistled she
> would respond by head jerking and running
> over to the fence to locate me. A recording
> was made of my whistle, and when [it was]
> played at the front of the cage she responded
> in the same manner as if I were there (DePrato,
> "Twentieth Century Dragons").

Johnny Arnett, Area Supervisor of Reptiles, Amphibians, and Fish, at the Cincinnati Zoological and
Botanical Garden, discovered that, by the time his shy
specimens had been at the zoo six months, they had
learned to retreat to their cave at the sound of his whistle
because it meant he was about to enter their enclosure.
Arnett also reported that Wanita (Pretty Lady) and Naga
(Dragon) recognize him in a crowd of viewers on the
other side of the glass barrier, even when he is not
wearing his uniform (Arnett, 1990).

Keepers at the San Diego Zoo and the New York
Zoo have commented on the friendliness and tameness of
dragons they kept in the past, according to Michael
Goodwin, lead reptile keeper at the Cincinnati Zoo (1990).
He was also told that the Taronga Park Zoo dragon in
Sydney, Australia used to come running when its keeper

entered the cage, rubbed against him like a cat, and enjoyed being scratched behind the ears with the keepers' keys to help it shed dead skin. The last trait is comparable to pet iguanas, which will sit still to allow their owners to remove peeling skin from their jaws and sides. Not all zoo dragons are utterly tame, however, and various curators have reported that monitors of all species seem more likely to attack if they are kept in outside enclosures. Johnny Arnett (1990) reported being told of a keeper in Jakarta who was bitten on the hand, and another showed him scars on his arm from a previous bite. A third keeper had been bitten on the foot, which was so badly mangled he could no longer walk.

"She's gone after us several times, giving resistance to being pushed around," Johnny Arnett (1990) said of Wanita, whom he called the more "persnickety" of the two Cincinnati Zoo dragons. "Not once have they gone after me to attack."

Early Zoo Dragons

The Burden expedition's dragons, the first brought to the United States, did not survive long in captivity. They went on display in the Bronx Zoo in September, 1926, and one died a month later. The larger specimen, assumed to be male, was measured at 8 feet, 4 inches (2.5 m) when it died in November of that year, weighing only 100 pounds (45 kg). Although Dr. Auffenberg's study (1981) indicates this might be rather light but still normal for a healthy wild dragon, it was later learned that zoo dragons, in general, eat more regularly than those in the wild and tend to weigh more than their wild counterparts. In December of the same year, the only other dragon living outside of Indonesia died shortly after its arrival at the Amsterdam Zoo. This was the same animal described by Cobham in his letter to the *London Times* after he met it chained to a tree in Bima. In an unpublished manuscript which he prepared in 1964 for the National Zoo, Marvin Jones states that, according to a 1926 account, the dragon, which had attacked a horse while in Bima, was "hand tame" by the time it arrived in Amsterdam. However, that may have been the human interpretation of a dying animal's disregard for its environment.

The Burden expedition's field studies and collection of skeletons and skins provided scientists with valuable information about Komodo dragons, but the Bronx Zoo's benefits from the expedition were literally short-lived. Another, less-publicized expedition the following year was not intended to duplicate Dr. Dunn's herpetological studies, yet from zoological societies' point of view, it was much more valuable; yielding four of the longest lived early zoo dragons. They provided pioneer knowledge to keepers throughout the world, as well as entertaining thousands of zoogoers for a combined total of at least 52 "dragon years." H. R. Rookmaker, the assistant resident governor on Flores, organized the 1927 expedition to western Flores or to Rinca (accounts differ) which yielded six dragons. In tracing the history of these early exports, Marvin Jones found out the Dutch administrator gave a pair of dragons each to the visiting German herpetologist Robert Mertens, to the Berlin Zoological Gardens and Aquarium, and to the Surabaya Botanical and Zoological Gardens in Java.

The larger of the two dragons given to Dr. Mertens had been badly injured during capture and refused to eat, so it was put to sleep. This male dragon was later to prove the second largest dragon ever measured; Dr. Mertens measured him at 9 feet, 10 inches (3.004 m), though the tanned skin shrank to a smaller size. The female dragon, only 5 feet, 8 inches (1.75 m) long, survived well on butcher's scraps aboard ship during the return to Germany. Dr. Mertens presented Bubchen (Sweetie-Pie) to the Frankfurt Zoological Gardens, where she was given a home in the Aquarium. Translating a 1942 article by Gustav Lederer, Marvin Jones learned that the imitation tropical environment which the German zoo provided was kept at a constant 86° F (30° C), with the pool about 9° F (5° C) warmer. Bubchen was fond of a warm bath but refused to enter the water when it was too chilly for her standards. Her three months on butcher's scraps had reinforced her natural taste for red meat, but the keepers gradually weaned her from her initial zoo diet of horse meat to more easily stocked foods: pigeons, young chickens, rats, guinea pigs, rabbits, small fish, liver, and eggs.

It is noted that she was fed in experiment the eggs of other reptiles, which she ate with relish, and quite by accident a water lizard and a green lizard that entered her cage in error. When the rats were fed, it is noted that these were alternated, once alive and once dead, to keep her in "shape." Normally she was fed twice a week... (Jones, 1964).

Bubchen prospered in this setting, growing to 7 feet, 4 inches (2.2 m) and laying several clutches of eggs (though of course none were fertilized) during her 17 years in captivity. Though one of the largest female dragons ever recorded, she proved to be gentle in captivity, "cuddling up to a young lady keeper" for a photograph and willingly going on walks through the zoo grounds with anyone, although Dr. Priemel, the director, was apparently a favorite. She died of human causes at last, when an Allied air raid during World War II destroyed the aquarium.

Of the two dragons which H.R. Rookmaker donated to Berlin, the female soon died of unrecorded causes, but the 6 foot, 10.5 inch-long (2.10 m) male was particularly long-lived; like Bubchen in Frankfurt, he survived until 1944, when the fortunes of war also led to his death. The Berlin Aquarium was bombed in 1943, so the dragon was sent to Leipzig (along with other rare specimens), where he died of a sudden illness in early 1944. The dragon's size at the time of capture indicates he was a young adult of at least five years, so he may have been more than 22 years old when he died, measuring over a foot longer (2.42 m). Whether that is extremely old for a dragon has not yet been determined, though the Cincinnati Zoo estimates members of the species may live as long as 35 years (Maruska, 1990) and Dr. Auffenberg (1981) has suggested they may live to 50 years. Although the nature of the Berlin dragon's illness was not stated, perhaps it can be assumed that the sudden change of environment and probably of temperature was fatal for the mature animal.

The Surabaya Zoo, on the north central coast of Java near Buitenzorg (now Bogor), housed four dragons in its open-air terrarium by the time Dr. Mertens visited in 1928, of which two were H.R. Rookmaker's gifts. It is possible that when the Buitenzorg Botanical Gardens and Museum closed sometime before 1926, Dr. Ouwens' dragons—if they were still alive—were sent to Surabaya. The female dragon donated by H.R. Rookmaker laid eggs several times, but none of the clutches were fertilized. The first record of dragons mating in a zoo is 1937, when the same female dragon mated with a male added to the enclosure two years earlier. A lying-in room was provided so the female could dig a burrow, but none of the eggs she laid in August and December of that year were viable. E.L. Tanzer and Jhr.W.C. Heurn, whose 1938 article in *Treubia* recorded the above details, speculated that the soil condition and temperature were wrong for success-ful hatching. One egg proved to be missing, and—based on knowledge about the species acquired in later years—

it must be assumed that one of the adults ate it.

British and American Dragons

In the late 1920's and early 1930's, with England in the grip of the Great Depression, life in London must have been a dreary affair. Banks failed nationwide, and by 1932, more than one out of every ten employable adults was out of work. News from the Continent presaged the coming world war: from 1933 through 1935, Adolf Hitler became chancellor of Germany, dictators took over Austria and Bulgaria, Benito Mussolini's Italy conquered Ethiopia, and the Spanish Civil War began. Perhaps the best temporary escape from grim reality was a visit to the London Zoo to see two exotic and appealing inhabitants of the Reptile House.

Provided to the zoo by Dr. Malcolm Smith in June, 1927, Sumbawa and Sumba (named after two of the Lesser Sunda Islands near their homeland) developed quite a flair for the theatrical as they became tame. Dr. Loveridge (1945) and Marvin Jones (1964) separately compiled reminiscences about the popular zoo lizards. One dragon was docile around children, following Joan B. Proctor, the keeper, around and coming to eat when called. In her 1929 article in the zoo's journal, Proctor included a photograph of a young child stroking one of the dragons, which were both seven feet long (2.1 m) by then. Some of their antics were also filmed in 1929. Sumbawa would daintily eat eggs one at a time from a stout metal tablespoon — until the day she bit through the handle and swallowed the bowl of the spoon along with the egg. One of the two would also let Joan Proctor walk it around the compound, holding its tail like a leash or rudder.

Certainly a more tame individual could not have

existed than the animal described by Miss Proctor which was shown to a gathering of the Zoological Society of London, without even a leash. It walked down a table, ate a chicken, a pigeon and some eggs from Miss Proctor's hands, and even allowed one [guest] to pet it while eating, some thing which few animals will allow (Jones, 1964).

Despite this loving care, the London dragons were not terribly long-lived in comparison to Bubchen and the Berlin dragon. Sumbawa died in early 1934, while Sumba must have died sometime after fall, 1937, for he was still listed in the 1938 guide book, by then measuring a full 9 feet (2.7 m) in length. R.A. Lanworn, zoologist to the London Zoological Society, later reported that the zoo had their tame pair for 12 years, but he was apparently writing about events that occurred long before he joined the zoo staff; it is possible that the zoo's records confused Sumba and Sumbawa with the pair of dragons supplied in 1936 by the Lord Moyne expedition (Jones, 1964; Lanworn, 1972).

Turn on the television on a lazy Saturday morning and skip through the channels full of cartoons and old black and white movies in search of something interesting. Stop at a repeat episode of "Wild Kingdom," with white-haired host Marlin Perkins commenting from the banks of the Nile River about the crocodiles lounging before the camera. There is a measuring look in Marlin Perkins' eyes as he gazes at the largest "croc"; perhaps he is remembering another giant quadruped reptile which he encountered decades ago, the largest Komodo dragon ever recorded.

In 1932, when Marlin Perkins was curator of reptiles at the St. Louis, Missouri zoo, two volunteers — 22-year-old John S. Smith and his friend Prentice M. Miles — assisted at the reptile house before setting off on their own "wild kingdom" safari, a world trip to gather rare specimens for the St. Louis and Bronx zoos. Arriving on Java in 1933, they bought the largest of the Surabaya Zoo's five Komodo dragons for the then-princely sum of $500. Once they had gathered 150 other animals, the two young men booked passage on a Dutch freighter from Singapore to Los Angeles. Despite previous promises to the partners, the captain moored the ship off Alaska and cold weather killed many tropical snakes in the collection. The Komodo dragon, accustomed to equatorial temperatures, also fared poorly.

"Minnie the Dragon Lady," the sensationalist title given to the dragon after it arrived in St. Louis, measured 10 feet, 2.5 inches (3.06 m) a record that has never been topped, despite rumors of larger dragons. Undoubtedly a full grown male, Minnie was an overwhelming success during the two weeks he was exhibited at the St. Louis Zoo; according to the newspapers, one day's attendance at his display totalled 25,000. Unable to settle on a purchase price with Marlin Perkins' employers, John Smith and Prentice Miles were in the process of negotiating Minnie's appearance at the Chicago World's Fair when he died, scarcely two weeks after his arrival in the United States. Stuffed and mounted as a curiosity, Minnie drifted from owner to owner and was even displayed in a beer hall before ending up at the Tilden Regional Park near Berkeley, California. The story of Minnie's odyssey was detailed in an unpublished article by Monte Monteagle provided by Tilden Regional Park ranger Alan I. Kaplan (Monteagle, "The Komodo Dragon").

Another American expedition the next year set a different record: Griswold and Harkness caught 43 dragons in the course of their 1934 visit, but their permit only allowed them to keep eight. Marvin Jones (1964) reports that four were officially given to the Dutch colonial government, presumably for inclusion in the Surabaya

The largest Komodo ever captured (currently in
Tilden Regional Park, near Berkeley, California)

Photo courtesy of David Lutz

Zoo collection, three were given to the Bronx Zoo, and
one was donated to the National Zoo in Washington, D.C.
Unfortunately, the New York dragons' longevity was not
much better than that of previous American dragons:
despite force-feeding, one died within two weeks, while
the other two seemed to feed normally but both died
within five months of their arrival. The National Zoo
dragon also died in less than two years.

The de Jong Dragons

A wave of Komodo dragon collecting expeditions
set forth from numerous nations, primarily European, in
the years between the two world wars, yielding specimens for zoos ranging from Surabaya to Antwerp to New
York. Because Indonesia remained a Dutch colony until

after World War II, the Netherlands' capital city of Amsterdam seems to have had the best supplied European zoo in these early years. Among the many dragons owned by Amsterdam over the years, most notable were the three which arrived in 1930. One, a female, laid eggs a year after her arrival, but there is no record of whether breeding had taken place, and at any rate no young hatched. Both female dragons died in 1933, but the male lived in captivity for nine years (Jones, 1964).

Although complete chronicles of individual zoos' experiences are not generally available, the Royal Zoological Society of Antwerp, Belgium, published an article in 1965 that detailed the zoo's dragon keeping during the years 1930 through 1964. "The Problem of the Komodo Lizards" (Mortelmans and Vercruysse, 1965) begins with two dragons presented to the future King Leopold III by the Dutch East Indies government when he toured the country in 1930: unfortunately, one died aboard ship and the other lived for less than a year. Five of the seven dragons received by the Antwerp Zoo died in their first three years in captivity; in fact, three died within the first year. This total does not include the dragon which escaped overboard in 1937 during the voyage to Belgium nor the dragon acquired in 1958 and sent to the Frankfurt Zoo after six months, where, Marvin Jones (1964) states, it soon died of an infection. The two longest-lived Antwerp dragons both survived in captivity for six and a half years; the first died in a bomb attack in World War II, and the second succumbed, after a series of infections and problems, in 1964.

The largest single collection, the last made before World War II, was J.K. de Jong's 1937 expedition to Flores, and possibly also to Komodo, which yielded 19 specimens for the Zoological Garden of Batavia in Jakarta (de Jong, 1944; Jones, 1964). Because the Batavia Zoo of earlier days and the current Ragunan Zoo are both based in Jakarta, these zoos are referred to by name rather than by city. Dragons from the Batavia collection were to grace zoo collections worldwide, including those in Rome, Rotterdam, Edinburgh, Washington, D.C., and Philadelphia — and maybe even Amsterdam, Copenhagen, or Stockholm — while five remained in Jakarta. It is possible that the Antwerp dragon received in 1937 was also one of the de Jong dragons.

Two Batavia Zoo dragons from that expedition flourished in Java's warm climate for 4 1/2 years, hatching the first successful captive-born dragons in April of 1941, although the two hatchlings died in the same year (de Jong, 1944). The parents were killed in January, 1942, just before Japan invaded Indonesia during World War II. Neither Marvin Jones nor Dr. de Jong specify whether the dragons were killed as food or to prevent their escaping and running wild during the invasion.

There is allegedly in existence a paper written by a Japanese army officer during the war. This paper proposes the capture of Komodo dragons and their release behind Allied lines. Fortunately, this was never done and the authors of this book were unable to verify the reality of the reported document. At any rate, the story provides another possible reason for the Indonesian zoo dragons to be killed by their keepers before the invasion.

Batavia zookeepers were astonished when approximately 25 dragons hatched in the supposedly empty cage in June, 1941. Dragons' eggs incubate for 8 to 8 1/2 months, and the keepers had not thought to search for buried eggs. In 1945, 15 of these captive-born dragons were still alive, although two had been sent to Tokyo's zoo during the course of the war (de Jong, 1947; Jones, 1964) One of the captive-born dragons was later moved to the Surabaya Zoo, where it lived for at least 20 years; in 1959 it was only 5 feet (1.5 m) in length, but by 1962 it had

Mating (Surabaya Zoo)

Photo courtesy of Surabaya Zoo

Laying eggs

Photo courtesy of Surabaya Zoo

grown to 6 feet, 6 inches (2 m.). Marvin Jones (1964)
speculated that a dragon that remained so small after 20
years must be female.

He also states that Philadelphia kept one of the de
Jong dragons for two years and another for five before
they died. When they arrived at the zoo the dragons were
only interested in eating eggs, but for some reason it was
decided to wean them to a pure horse-meat diet; perhaps
the zookeepers felt the red meat was closer to the dragons' natural foods. The dragons were correctly identified
as a mateable pair, both measuring 7 feet, 6 inches (2.25 m)
in length. The female dragon was the longest female ever
recorded but she may have been too big for the male to
properly restrain during any breeding attempts. Unfortunately, little information about the pair survives.

Two dragons from the de Jong collection were
also destined for Washington, D.C., but one escaped
overboard during the trip. The other dragon arrived
safely and lived for 12 years in a 32-foot by 12-foot (9.6 m
by 3.6 m) indoor cage, setting the record for dragon
longevity in the Western hemisphere. Curator Mario
DePrato later reported that, with no automatic thermo-
stat in the cage, keepers opened and shut ventilators to
regulate temperature. The dragon would climb onto the
cement-enclosed radiators and sit on the grates to stay
warm, but when it slid down off the radiator its tail would
hit the concrete floor and the tip eventually broke off.
Smaller, thin-tailed lizards of many other species may
lose their tails when caught, but losing a tail tip is as
painful and unnatural for monitors as it is for cats, and the
injury never healed (DePrato, "Twentieth Century
Dragons").

Modern Dragon Keeping

After Indonesia proclaimed its independence in

1945 and completed the revolution in 1949, the country was absorbed in the political problems of developing a new government. Nonetheless, word may have reached the government of a failed American collecting expedition: animal dealer Wyman Carrol unsuccessfully attempted to capture some dragons in 1956, but he was evacuated from Komodo Island with a dragon bite and no specimens (Jones, 1964). Nineteen fifty-six was also the year that David Attenborough arrived to make a film about Komodo Island for the British Broadcasting Corporation (BBC). Although he did not collect any zoo specimens, Attenborough increased the dragon's popularity with the outside world, due to his film and a later book about the expedition.

That year, President Sukarno ruled that dragon collecting was to be limited to 12 monitors every three years (King, 1968). At some point it was also decided that only Indonesian zoo experts would be allowed to collect Komodo dragons, and that these zoos in turn would provide dragons for foreign zoos.

In 1955, the Surabaya Zoo provided the Bronx Zoo with two dragons, supposedly a mateable pair since one was almost twice the size of the other, but when one died the same year and the second in 1959, both proved to be male. The San Diego Zoological Gardens also received two dragons from the Surabaya Zoo in August, 1963, but one died in late 1963 and the other in early 1964, and curators discovered that they too were both males. Access to eastern hemisphere dragon-keeping records for recent years is difficult to obtain; however, Marvin Jones noted in his 1964 manuscript that two dragons arrived at the Antwerp Zoo in 1958, an egg-laying female was given to Frankfurt in 1961, and another dragon was donated to the zoological gardens in Basel, Switzerland in 1962 (Jones, 1964). How long they each survived in captivity is unclear.

Since at least 1964, any dragons exported from Indonesia are officially provided as a gift from the Indonesian people to the people of the recipient nation, through the medium of their two governments. For example, when, after a period of negotiation, the National Zoological Park in Washington, D.C., received two Surabaya Zoo dragons in 1964, Director Theodore Reed officially accepted the dragons on behalf of the United States government. Several years later, after the male dragon had died, Indonesia's President and Mrs. Soeharto toured the National Zoo and offered to provide a second male dragon, which arrived in 1970 (DePrato, "Twentieth Century Dragons").

According to the Komodo Monitor Consortium in 1983, the Taronga Park dragon in Sydney, Australia had at that date survived in captivity for more than 20 years, but it is not clear whether the dragon is still alive. Six captive-bred hatchlings arrived in Basel in 1968, where they grew to adulthood and one was later sent to the San Diego Zoo. (Bacon et al, 1983) Xeroxed articles from the Cincinnati Zoo indicate that the Surabaya Zoo provided two female dragons (at first thought to be a pair) to the San Diego Zoo in 1968, and the 7 foot, 6 inch (2.25 m) male dragon from the Basel Zoo arrived in San Diego in 1976. When the 20-year-old male dragon died in 1986, "Sunshine" — the surviving 18-year-old female — was the only living dragon in the Western Hemisphere, but she died within a year.

In 1986, when President Ronald Reagan visited the island of Bali, President Soeharto presented him with two Komodo dragons as a gift to the people of the United States. Nearly two years later, all the necessary permits had been obtained and Dr. Dale Marcellini, curator of reptiles at the National Zoo, and Bela Demeter, a keeper in the zoo's Reptile House, collected the specimens from the Ragunan Zoo in Java.

In 1988, Ed Maruska, director of the Cincinnati Zoo, also visited Indonesia to discuss the possibility of a dragon donation, which was arranged after an official presentation of two dragons from President Soeharto to President Bush in 1990. In the spring of 1990, Johnny Arnett collected the new dragons from the Ragunan Zoo. Dr. Maruska (1990) reports that the Singapore Zoo also has a large, healthy pair of dragons and he believes there is a dragon in the Berlin Zoo as well. San Diego Zoo representatives, at the time this book went to press, were in the process of negotiating for the arrival of a new pair of dragons. Today, both Ragunan and Surabaya Zoos have flourishing dragon populations and both are successful in raising dragons born in captivity. Contributing to the zoos' success is both their long history of caring for dragons and the climate, which is similar to the dragons' native environment. At present, no dragons have been captive-born outside of Indonesia, although the female dragon currently in the National Zoo has laid clutches three times after mating with the male.

Modern Care and Breeding of Dragons

Before many field studies of the Komodo dragons had been done, zoo curators had to guess at the appropriate temperatures and foods to use, and dragons in captivity were forced to adjust to sometimes drastic changes in their environment and diet. Time and again, zoos received new specimens and — with few exceptions — lost them to illness or parasitic infection within a few years after acquisition. This was not the result of neglect so much as it was an indication of how little was known about maintaining exotic reptiles, especially Komodo dragons, in captivity. Collecting dragons was one thing, but keeping them was another.

[Komodo dragons] have often arrived there [in zoos] in poor condition with cankered jaws, septic feet, or afflicted by abcesses. Careful treatment, however, supplemented by artificial sunlight and a tropical temperature, has been successful in restoring them to health (Loveridge, 1945).

In "Twentieth Century Dragons," Mario DePrato detailed how the older dragon cage, which had housed the de Jong dragon from 1937 through 1949, was refurbished before the new dragons arrived in 1964. The room was completely reworked, with the radiators laid on their sides and covered with cement to provide warm mounds which the dragons could climb on and off without difficulty. Copper rods were installed under the rest of the floor to ensure radiant heat, while temperature controls and sun lamps gave the keepers an opportunity to vary the warmth of the environment to imitate day and night temperatures in the wild.

As an island species, the Komodo dragon had not been exposed to many of the parasites and diseases to which continental reptiles build up a resistance. Although they may not encounter too many unfamiliar microbes in the zoos on Java, dragons moved to the northern hemisphere are easily subject to infections and parasites, much more serious than the ticks that several zoos have found when their specimens arrived from Indonesia. An example is the Antwerp Zoo dragon which died in 1959 of respiratory problems: the autopsy showed tumors throughout the dragon's trachea and bronchial tubes had cut off his breathing, but the tumors themselves were caused by larvae of the parasitic worms which infested his bronchial tubes (Mortelmans and Vercruysse, 1965).

DePrato reported that, in 1964, the National Zoo's male dragon caught his toe on a projection and pulled the toenail off, exposing the bone, and the entire toe had to be removed. Apparently due to the cement floor, the dragon also developed numerous cracks on his footpads, but died of an amoebic infection before a dirt floor could be installed. Partially in response to the problems encountered with the male dragon, the National Zoo soon established an outdoor exhibit where Renee could live from June through September each year. A large water fowl enclosure was converted, allowing her to receive ample fresh air and sunshine in the daytime while spending her nights in a hut with heat coils installed beneath the floor. Her new mate once scraped off four osteoderms (skin bones), leaving deep holes that did not heal all winter, despite medication. Once the dragon was moved to the outside enclosure for the summer, however, the wounds healed nicely due to exposure to fresh air and sunshine. (DePrato, "Twentieth Century Dragons")

In 1990, the Cincinnati Zoo learned it would soon acquire its first pair of Komodo dragons. The Ragunan Zoo had kept the dragons primarily in an outdoor enclosure since their capture as youngsters six years before. In addition to providing an external home for the summer months, the Cincinnati Zoo staff converted a 10 by 40 foot (3 by 12 m) special exhibit cage to mirror the animals' natural habitat, both in appearance and in temperature. A painted backdrop recreates the Komodo Island landscape from photographs and heat lamps give the space a golden glow. The enclosure includes a simulated beach, a swimming pool, a feeding area, and two "caves" whose back doors each lead to a concrete-floored holding tank lined with fuller's earth. After learning all they could about the National Zoo's current thermoregulatory techniques, the Cincinnati Zoo's technical operations staff prepared the heating system. The enclosure's palm plants look impossibly fake in downstate Ohio, even indoors, but in fact the plants are real and the craggy-looking basking rocks are imitations.

> They're actually manmade, an increasingly common technique that uses gunnite, a form of cement, on a wire frame. To allow the zoo's rocks to "retain" and radiate heat, designers called for pePEX [polyethlene] tubing to be wound on the wire structures before the gunnite was sprayed on (Kaeter, 1990).

As detailed in a publication of the heating system company, the entire habitat had to be able to maintain 100° F (38° C) heat, even in winter, with varying climate zones ranging from 75° to 110° F (24° to 43° C). Underground radiant heating tubes of pePEX, designed to make the dragons feel they are on a sun-warmed beach, were installed beneath several feet of "dirt"; a pebbly layer was spread on top to further reduce the chances of possible wounds becoming infected. Sensors within the polyethlene tubing in the ground and rocks now determine when the optimum temperature is reached and close down the supply of hot water running through the tubes. Keepers can also vary the temperature from rock to rock as needed (Kaeter, 1990).

Apparently the Cincinnati pair finds the enclosure acceptable because in early June, shortly after their arrival at the zoo, Michael Goodwin observed the dragons in courtship behavior, although they may not actually have mated. The usually alert dragons did not notice the keeper for several minutes as he looked through the viewing window of their enclosure.

> Initially the male was lying on the female with his tail noticeably arched. I could not see

the female's tail because of their position in the enclosure...and because the male's tail obstructed my view. The male then began 'nosing' or 'nuzzling' [the] female with his snout behind and under her forelegs, neck, and head while his tongue flicked in and out over her skin as if "tasting" her. The male also scratched or clawed [the] female on her back near her back legs and also near her shoulder region above the forelegs. During the entire encounter the female remained passive with her head held flat against the ground. ...[The] female did not move even when scratched roughly. Suddenly the male noticed my presence, stared at me, and discontinued his activity with the female (Goodwin, 1990).

In early December, apparent mating behavior was again noticed, and a few weeks later Wanita began digging a burrow. Since this is often a sign that a female plans to lay eggs, Naga was separated from her. Digging with her front paws, she would toss the dirt up behind her as far as 3 to 5 feet (.9 to 1.5 m), according to Michael Dulaney, a zoo supervisor, who photographed her actions. Over a period of four hours, she dug the burrow so deep that she could crawl all the way into it except for her tail. During the process of digging, she would occasionally stop and circle the exhibit or simply rest, splayed out on the ground with her head on a nearby rock. She dug upward and created enough of a second entrance to stick her head out, but when the burrow collapsed Wanita showed no further interest in burrowing and her mate was returned to the exhibit (Dulaney, 1990).

Food for the Dragons

Dr. Lanworn (1972) reports that a friend traveling to Surabaya Zoo before World War II discovered the dragons "were fed largely on the town's pariah dogs" and apparently stayed healthy on such a diet. The major difference between the two Indonesian zoos and western zoos is that in Indonesia the dragons are consistently fed live animals and remain outdoors much of the year. Because of the suitable climate and large outdoors facilities, both zoos keep more dragons than would be possible for the average zoo in the northern hemisphere.

In addition to her regular diet, the National Zoo's Renee found several opportunities to eat live prey when, at various times in the late 1960's, a squirrel, a pigeon, and a mallard duck and five ducklings wandered into her enclosure. Mario DePrato ("Twentieth Century Dragons") arrived in time to save a sixth duckling, and the mother duck was able to fly to safety. When the external dragon exhibit was built, in the summer of 1964, Renee and a Malayan water monitor *(V.salvator)* were put in the enclosure together. The dragon prowled the exhibit constantly, ignoring the other monitor, which spent most of its time in the hut. However, a month and a half later, halfway through a month-long hunger strike, Renee "grabbed the monitor by the neck and held on, rendering it helpless." When zookeepers separated the two, it took 37 stitches to close the wound on the Malayan monitor's neck; despite antibiotic treatment, it died 5 1/2 months later.

> Food consisted of the following: meat and intestines of deer, sheep, goat, peccary, and gazelle; also fed rabbits, horse meat, horse liver, and horse hearts. ...The female was also offered baby chicks, of which she ate only one. They would tickle her

nose and she would shake her head and refused to eat any more of them. Another time, she was fed three small rabbits... She retained these for 5 1/2 hours, then regurgitated them. Then she tore them up and re-ate all of the pieces (DePrato, "Twentieth Century Dragons").

Similarly, Johnny Arnett reported that when Cincinnati's Wanita goes off her feed, he provides a special meal of beef organs such as lung, spleen, kidneys and heart, which she gorges, regurgitates, and re-eats. This trait, also seen in the wild, may be a method of repositioning the food in the throat, since — like snakes — dragons cannot chew and must swallow their food whole. Mario DePrato also reports that, when eating whole rabbits, the National Zoo dragons would move their heads and necks from side to side to reposition the prey before swallowing it.

Naga and Wanita are fed every seven to ten days, based on the leanness of their bellies and how much they ate at the previous feeding. This schedule was developed as a result of Dr. Auffenberg's advice not to overfeed the dragons. The pair's primary diet in Jakarta was kangaroo meat and chickens, but in Ohio, Naga and Wanita are fed a much more varied diet, including chickens, quail, guinea fowl, and laboratory rats and mice. In the arid eastern Indonesia environment, dragons derive almost all their moisture intake from the blood and fluids of the animals they eat. At Dr. Auffenberg's suggestion, the Cincinnati Zoo provides its animals with bloody red meat with the bones intact, such as goat meat and road-killed deer provided by the Ohio Department of Natural Resources. In addition, during hunting season, some hunters provide the zoo with organ meat from the deer they have killed. Johnny Arnett rounds out their diet with five pounds of caplan (a smelt-like fish) per feeding (Arnett, 1990).

6

TROUBLE IN PARADISE

As early as 1866, biologist Joseph Hooker detailed the advantages and limitations of being an insular, or island, species. In *The Flight of the Iguana*, David Quammen (1988) discussed Dr. Hooker's theories in terms of the Galapagos Islands, but most points can also be applied to Wallacean islands. As explained in Chapter 4, the dragons had dwindled in size and range from their gigantic beginnings as ocean-dwelling mosasaurs and prehistoric Australia-roaming *Megalania*, but they were still a hardy species when they made the "long pioneer crossings of salt water" that every island immigrant must undergo. Their dispersal ability enabled them to make the journey and survive unknown millennia of island-hopping as Komodo and the other nearby islands achieved their current form. Even though the sinking of sections of the Komodo land mass in the last 20,000 years probably cut the dragons' range in half (Auffenberg, 1981), isolation in this ideal ecological niche and freedom from other large predators allowed the dragons to flourish.

> The isolation compels an inbreeding popula-
> tion to shape themselves, genetically, toward
> the new challenges of this new island habitat;
> and the escape from predators and competi-
> tors allows that same population a great lati-
> tude of experiment, transformation, aggran-
> dizement (Quammen, 1988).

It seems possible that before they reached Komodo, dragons were smaller monitors who could swim much better than the modern *V. komodoensis*. The very traits that made it possible for them to reach the Lesser Sunda Islands disappeared over the generations when they proved unnecessary for island survival. Komodo drag-ons can still swim well, traveling underwater over 300 feet (100 m) at a time before surfacing for air (Auffenberg, 1981), but in general the species is much less fond of water than several other monitor species. Now that Australia's continental shelf has sunk, the ocean that brought the dragons to Wallacea is the barrier that prevents them from leaving.

At its present size, the Komodo dragon species would be handicapped if it attempted to migrate even to such relatively nearby large islands as Sulawesi or Sumbawa. It might be possible to swim the distance, but large mammalian predators have already filled the eco-logical niche occupied by dragons on Komodo. If the dragons were smaller and had retained their affinity for water, they could have spread as far as the Malayan water monitor *V. salvator*, which spends much of its time in the water and is content to live off of smaller mammals, other reptiles, and birds' eggs. While the Komodo dragon's entire wild population remains restricted to a handful of small islands, the Malayan monitor lives on almost every Sunda Island except those occupied by the Komodo monitors. In fact, the Malayan monitor's range on Flores overlaps with that of the Komodo dragon. By the time the first humans settled on Komodo Island sometime before 1911, the dragons were firmly entrenched on their six small islands and the southwestern coast of Flores; they could not migrate away from their changing paradise.

Viewing the Dragons

The experience of encountering dragons on Komodo Island has changed considerably since the Burden expedition released five dragons on the beach of Telok Slawi (Python Bay) to see if they would run into the jungle or swim away. Since Dr. Auffenberg's field study, most expeditions to Komodo have been primarily for the sake of viewing the animals rather than scientifically studying them. Dr. Auffenberg himself had several less-than-scientific encounters with a particularly bad-tempered dragon.

> When I met him [the large adult dragon tagged as 34-W] on a game trail, this individual would approach with mouth open and tail bowed in threat. He once stalked my children on the beach and often came directly into our camp. On one occasion he drove us out of our tent, stuck his head into a knapsack, removed a shirt and tore it to shreds. There was no question in our minds that if given the opportunity this animal would attack, whether provoked or not (Auffenberg, 1981)

Although researchers on Komodo sometimes tethered live goats to study how dragons attack their prey, they learned to hang carrion from a tree to attract more dragons in a shorter period of time. Usually they used a goat killed three days before using it as prey.

When F. Wayne King visited Komodo in 1968, scientists had been using the Vai Liang (now called Banu Gulang) ravine as their trapping site for at least a dozen years (King, 1968), and the dragons knew that it was a good place to search for dead goats hung up by humans. Dr. Auffenberg used similar bait at five separate trapping sites during his 1969-1970 field study (Auffenberg, 1981). As tourist expeditions increased, the dragons learned to congregate at one spot in Banu Gulang whenever people approached the gully, because it indicated they were about to be fed. Using an older, smellier carcass to attract the dragons was no longer necessary. Instead, the dragons were fed whenever a group of tourists brought a goat to be slaughtered and hung above the ten-foot (3 m) deep ravine. Tourists now watch the dragons from a fenced viewing area above the gully.

The feeding arena is about 30 minutes' walk from the ranger station and visitor compound over a level and relatively wide path. Tourists are not allowed to walk on this path, nor elsewhere on the island, without a guide. This is a sensible regulation since dragons are occasionally seen on the path. Komodo villagers breed goats for their own use and also to be fed to the dragons when the tourists arrive. On January 1, 1989, the National Park Service (PHPA) decreed the dragons should be fed a single goat and then only on Sunday; apparently, the park service now buys the goats from the villagers.

> To our left was a kind of bandstand. Several
> rows of bench seats were banked up behind
> each other, with a sloping wooden roof to
> protect them from the sun and other inclem-
> encies in the weather. Tied to the front rail of
> the bandstand were both ends of a long piece
> of blue nylon rope which ran out and down
> into the gully, where it was slung over a

pulley wheel which hung from the branches of a small bent tree. A small iron hook [to hold the dead goat] hung from the rope (Adams and Carwardine, 1990).

The viewing area and the path leading to it are surrounded by a two-foot-tall fence, which is wooden in some places and chicken wire in others. When Johnny Arnett (1990) visited the island on a weekday, one dragon climbed the slope of the gully at a point where the fence ended and sniffed around, apparently wondering why no goat had been provided. Seeing a group of humans standing together, it turned away without incident, as shown in a videotape made by a member of the group. Several dozen dragons live around the feeding arena and apparently subsist primarily on this artificial feeding. The remaining thousands of dragons on Komodo and the other islands do not participate in this 'show'.

Dragon feeding frenzy

Photo courtesy of Dr. Ed Maruska

As early as 1968, Hilmi Oesman of the Surabaya Zoo's board of directors discovered that once dragons are intent upon their feeding, it is relatively safe to approach them.

Hilmi told us it was not necessary to construct a blind from which to photograph the monitors, because once they start feeding they pay little attention to their surroundings. He said you could simply crawl close enough to take any photograph you wanted, or even to measure them with a steel tape (King, 1968).

Dr. King took Hilmi Oesman's advice and came within 10 feet (3 m) of the dragons, reporting that it was not fear of the dragons but repulsion at the stench of the three-day-old carrion goat that prevented him from coming closer. Knowing how dragons focus all their interest on their food while eating, rangers will sometimes let eager zoo representatives and photographers enter the feeding arena while the dragons are occupied: Dr. Phillips of the San Diego Zoo, Dr. Maruska of the Cincinnati Zoo, and Douglas Adams all report going into the gully during the dragons' mealtime. This was done at the rangers' suggestion although official park regulations forbid this practice. Johnny Arnett of the Cincinnati Zoo maintains that Dick and Mary Lutz placed their lives in jeopardy by entering the arena on a day when no food had been provided.

Because even the shortest boat trip to Komodo from Labuan Bajo can be a six-hour round trip, visitors must expect to stay overnight. The PHPA provides rustic accommodations for visitors: a series of stilted wooden buildings having a total of 38 bedrooms with shared but clean indoor plumbing. The open air cafeteria features a limited menu — rice, noodles, and beer — though tourists can bring other food, such as live chickens, which the cook will prepare for dinner.

Territorial Invasion

A dragon born on Komodo Island before the turn of the century might well spend the first 15 years of its life without encountering a human being. By that time, the 9-foot-long (2.7 m) solitary male has grown to dominate the other dragons in its "turf," sometimes eating the eggs of its own species and more than once killing and eating a year-old relative that did not escape up a tree in time. Although, like the others of its species, this dragon prefers scavenging to killing fresh prey, hunger and opportunity can easily move it to action. Deer and wild pigs are particular favorites, and it can kill and eat an animal in less than 20 minutes, unless other dragons arrive to quarrel over the feast. This dragon is in its prime and may live and grow longer for another 20 years or more before dying of natural causes, for as an adult it has no natural predators outside of its own species.

Then, over the course of the next several years, the dragon becomes aware of a new element in the island's food chain. Strange smelling bipeds walk erect over the island, building their nests together in a single unnatural clump near the ocean. Hunting in groups rather than alone, the new species begins harvesting the rich crop of wildlife which is the dragon's food source. Since they are uninterested in carrion, except to bury it, the biped mammals make inroads on the island's plentiful supply of live game. Every adult dragon naturally smells out and hurries to other dragons' kills, so perhaps this individual's first encounter with the intruders is over a deer or pig which the humans have just killed. Driven away by their weapons, the dragon learns not to approach bipeds gathered in large groups, but — since it is accustomed to considering every species, even its own, as a source of food — before long the dragon attacks a lone human who walks into its hunting range.

> The drawback for any species in having evolved on an island, under conditions of isolation and escape, is that eventually the isolation is breached and the escape comes to a rude end. ...Suddenly, then, forms of anatomy and behavior that have served well for a million years may become, instead, under new circumstances, disastrous. ...All at once there are unfamiliar predators (or competitors, or maybe just parasites or disease organisms) sharing the island, and those newcomers present a threat with which the native species are not prepared to cope (Quammen, 1988).

Many authors, with only several paragraphs or a chapter to devote to the subject, call the Komodo dragons "man-eaters" and feel they have compressed a great deal of information into a single word. The problem with this sort of descriptive shorthand is that it does not take into consideration the natural state of predator animals. An elephant in danger or trying to protect its young can — and will — trample and kill people, but elephants are not generally considered killer animals. Both jackals and carrion birds eat human corpses, but the adjective "man-eating" is not usually included in their descriptions. Occasionally a tiger living near a human settlement will "go rogue" and begin hunting humans, yet the tiger as a species is not believed to be a natural predator of humans. In *Dangerous to Man*, Roger Caras (1975) identifies only two animals as natural hunters of humans: sharks and saltwater crocodiles. Shark fanciers would further specify that less than one-third of the 150 known shark species are dangerous to humans. The only dangerous lizards listed by Roger Caras are Gila monsters and Mexican beaded lizards, the two poisonous lizard species.

Komodo dragons are entirely carnivorous animals and, to a scavenger species, a human corpse is no more sacred than that of any other dead animal. Dragons are as capable as other scavengers of digging up graves in search of a meal. While the armchair traveler may shudder at this image, the people of Komodo have learned to be practical. They bury their dead quickly and pile sharp rocks on the graves or seal them with clay. Prevented from easy access to corpses in human settlements, dragons will not hesitate to eat dead humans that they encounter in the wild. There are at least two known cases from Komodo's history where the clues, or lack of clues, indicate one or more dragons ate a human that had just died.

In 1956, hunters from the neighboring island of Sumbawa left a very sick member of their group in the wilderness overnight, and returned with Komodo villagers the next day to find the man's arms, legs, and viscera consumed (Auffenberg, 1981). The other incident occurred in 1974, when a group of German tourists left an elderly Swiss man behind to rest under a tree while they completed their hike across the hilly terrain of Komodo. The party returned two hours later, but found no trace of Rudolf von Reding Biberegg other than his camera. An extensive, two-day search of the entire island yielded no more clues (Watson, 1987). A solitary cross, marked with a commemorative plaque, was erected on the sight where the Swiss baron was last seen, an hour's walk from the visitors compound.

IN MEMORY OF
Baron Rudolf von Reding Biberegg,
Born in Switzerland the 8 August 1895,
and disappeared on this island the
10th July, 1974,
'he loved nature throughout his life'.

Although the plaque refers to the baron disap-
pearing, it is generally believed that he was eaten by
dragons. Since dragons easily consume the hooves and
horns of other animals, the baron's clothes and shoes
were undoubtedly eaten as well.

To the human mind, one crucial question naturally
arises: did these two men die before the dragons found
them? The sick hunter may have succumbed of natural
causes, and the 79-year-old baron may have died of a
heart attack or heat stroke before the first dragon arrived.
Due to the lack of evidence, the question can never be
totally resolved. Even though Komodo dragons are not
natural hunters of humans, they will take advantage of an
opportunity such as both of these cases may have presented. The species are solitary predators, so any image
of a marauding pack of dragons must be dispelled, but a
single dragon could easily have killed a person sitting or
lying down, unarmed and unprepared for the assault.
Encountering a sick or sleeping human in a remote section of the island, any hungry adult dragon would react
precisely as it would to an injured animal — by killing it.

"I don't think anyone [any able-bodied adult] that
is cognizant of the animal could ever be hurt by the
Komodo [dragon]. Their whole success and strategy is in
ambush," said Cincinnati Zoo Director Ed Maruska (1990)
in a personal interview. Dr. Maruska entered the feeding
arena on Komodo Island during his 1988 trip and photographed the dragons as they were eating. He was accom-

panied by a guide equipped with a forked "dragon stick" to turn aside any interested dragon, as another guide did when a dragon approached Dick Lutz in the feeding arena in 1989. The person holding the dragon stick uses it to catch the dragon's neck and shoulders in the "Y" of the stick and hold it at arm's length. Dr. Maruska felt that he was in little danger because the dragons were more interested in the already-killed prey in front of them than in attacking two healthy adult humans already aware of their presence.

"Except in very rare and unusual circumstances I doubt that a Komodo [dragon] would attack a human," concurred Dale Marcellini, curator of herpetology at the National Zoo in Washington, D.C. in a letter to Dick Lutz. "Certainly the animals in zoos are not at all dangerous unless provoked."

Fatal Attacks

The Cincinnati Zoo estimates that a dozen people or more have been killed by dragons in the last 20 years; this is the highest estimate encountered by either author during research for this book, but fatalities resulting from Komodo dragon attacks have never been well-documented. Because the dragons' range is in one of the most remote and unpopulated regions of Indonesia, there are no written records of dragon-caused deaths in the early years of the twentieth century, if any occurred. News is still passed on by word of mouth in the small villages and towns of the Lesser Sunda Islands, since newspapers are the products of big cities, and the nation's 15 to 36 percent illiteracy rate must be much higher in the remote and poor regions of the archipelago. (The country's literacy rate is 64 percent, according to the 1988 World Almanac, although the U.S. State Department's Bureau of Public Affairs stated in an April, 1989 newsletter that the literacy rate in 1988 was 85 percent.) Western researchers have found that they must collect stories not only verbatim but often second-hand; there are seldom eye witnesses because dragons are not known to attack crowds of humans. Both animal and human survivors of dragon attacks are subject to two subsequent threats to their lives: they may die from loss of blood or the wound may become infected and eventually result in death. During his field study of the dragons, Dr. Auffenberg (1981) heard the report of a Komodo Island teenager who bled to death in 1931 after a dragon attacked him. According to the boy's father, telling the story more than thirty years after it happened, the father and his two sons were cutting wood in the forest and they jumped up and ran when a dragon approached. The 14-year-old boy became entangled in a vine and was mauled on the buttocks by the dragon, bleeding to death in less than half an hour. Presumably, the family was within the dragon's hunting range and it considered the youngest, smallest human to be easy prey.

Another fatal attack occured in 1947, when a visiting policeman from Flores reached down to pet a dragon kept by a Komodo villager. The dragon lunged upward and tore out the man's biceps; one week later, the policeman died in the Ruteng hospital on Flores of a severe infection (Auffenberg, 1981). A third story was reported to English naturalist David Attenborough (1984) several months after it happened in 1957. According to the village chief of Komodo, a man tripped over a dragon lying motionless in the grass and the dragon struck back with its tail "knocking the man over and numbing his legs so that he was unable to escape." The dragon mauled the man, whose wounds were so severe that he died soon after his fellow villagers found him.

In both cases, the dragon apparently interpreted the human's behavior as aggressive, if not an outright attack. The fallen man, once he was on the ground at the same level as the dragon, was particularly vulnerable to further attack.

Even in quite recent times, there are often only sketchy reports about human deaths caused by Komodo dragons. Dr. Auffenberg (1981) mentions a Flores resident who died two years after being bitten by a dragon, and he also wrote of two tourists killed between the time he left the island in 1973 and the time his book was completed in 1981. One of these deaths was probably that of Baron Biberegg, but no details were given about the other death. Although they do not cite their source nor the date of the supposed event, Douglas Adams and Mark Carwardine (1990) refer to the "well-known case" of a Frenchman who died of an infected wound in Paris, two years after being bitten by a dragon. Several other unsubstantiated stories were also encountered in the course of research.

Lyall Watson referred to a young, athletic Frenchman supposedly killed on Komodo in 1986, leaving behind only a blood-stained shoe (Watson, 1987). Johnny Arnett (1990) of the Cincinnati Zoo mentioned in conversation that a Ragunan Zoo keeper told him a tourist was killed in 1989, leaving no trace but his glasses.

Whether all of these stories have a basis in truth and how many human deaths have actually been caused by dragons may be impossible to determine. Although modern news media exist in Java and other far-distant Indonesian cities, it is unlikely that any newspaper office is located closer than, perhaps, Ruteng on the island of Flores. No effort seems to have been made to publicize any recent deaths.

Although the practice of building homes on stilts is a regional Indonesian tradition that pre-dates dragon contact, it has also proved useful in keeping humans out of the dragons' reach when they are most vulnerable (sick or sleeping). As early as 1965, Lyall Watson (1987) noticed that Komodo villagers never tethered their goats, for fear they would be unable to run away from hunting dragons (Watson, 1987). Photographs and first-hand accounts also indicate dragons wander into Kampung Komodo, usually in search of chickens, but Bela Demeter noted that the dragons rarely raided the village since the frequently provided goat carrion kept them well-fed (Demeter, 1988).

In early 1987, however, the inevitable occurred when a 6-year-old Rinca village boy playing in his family's yard or on the steps to the house was attacked and killed by a dragon. Rangers on Komodo showed Dick and Mary Lutz photographs of the dead child, badly bitten on the chest and the right thigh. It is obvious that the dragon found the small, solitary human a tempting target.

Recent accounts of people surviving dragon attacks include a woman bitten on Rinca in 1985 and a farmer attacked on Flores in August, 1989. An Indonesian government official in Labuan Bajo reported the first account to Dick and Mary Lutz. Adams and Carwardine (1990) stated that they met a Komodo Island woman who survived a dragon attack and underwent intensive surgery in Bali to avoid having her leg amputated. This may be the same case with the island names confused or perhaps the woman is a permanent inhabitant of Rinca whose family moves to Komodo for the fishing season. The more recent attack took place when a farmer in the reserve of Wai Wuul, just south of Labuan Bajo, heard his dog barking in the evening, went out to investigate, and was attacked. The farmer was not fatally injured.

A Species Endangered

In the fall of 1989, Dick and Mary Lutz entered a modest hotel in Bima, on the island of Sumbawa, and spoke with the owner, a self-sufficient woman born to a different way of life. In her face, royal bearing (Dick and Mary Lutz referred to her as 'the princess') and quick smile seem to be a reflection of her father, the man who took the first step to save Komodo dragons from human exploitation.

It was 1915, just a few years after the Komodo dragon came from myth to scientifically verified reality, when Nj. Djauhara Salahuddin's father, the Sultan of Bima, issued an edict protecting the newly discovered species. The Sultan's authority included eastern Sumbawa, Komodo, and the western third of the nearby island of Flores. The Sultan's ruling lasted until that tiny Manggarai District of the Sultanate was absorbed by authorities on the larger Timor Island to the south in 1924.

Also in 1915, the Dutch colonial government declared the Komodo dragon's range closed to hunters and limited the number of specimens which zoological expeditions could obtain (Dunn, 1927b).

Dr. Dunn and Douglas Burden reported that, despite the native and Dutch laws protecting the Komodo dragon, there had been "a certain amount" of poaching in the early part of 1926 before their arrival, with poachers and trappers taking "a good many skins" even though the bumpy scales known as osteoderms made the skins useless as a leather product (Burden, 1927; 1928). At least 300 monitors were shot that year, 100 each from Komodo, Flores and Rinca, according to the records of Chinese merchants based on Sumbawa Island in 1926. The Chinese made "swimming medicine" from the poached monitors, believing that the lizards' swimming ability could be passed on to humans, and they used dragon tails to make burn medication (Auffenberg, 1981).

Establishing laws and enforcing them are not equally easy, and the history of Komodo dragon protection is occasionally a troubled one. Apparently, there was a lapse of legal protection for the species from 1924, when the new Self Government of Manggarai officially cancelled the Sultan's order, to 1926 when the Manggarai officials passed an ordinance making it illegal to catch or hunt dragons, take their skins or eggs, or disturb their nests. The ruling of the Self Government was confirmed by the Dutch Resident Governor of Timor in January, 1927. The authorities were now well aware of the poaching problem, and Komodo Island was made a wilderness reserve area by the Governor General of the Dutch East Indies colony in November, 1928.

It was 1930 when the Dutch government strengthened the anti-poaching law with a 250-florin fine for hunting or capturing the animals. The central government also backed this rule in its 1931 Regulations for the Protection of Wild Animals.

In 1938, the Self Government of Manggarai extended the Komodo dragons' wilderness reserve area to include southern Rinca and Padar islands. A warden was to be located in the town of Reo, on Flores Island, but the position was not actually filled until 30 years later, after President Soeharto took office. That the position needed filling cannot be denied, for in January 1939, half a year after Rinca and Padar were given protection, the Dutch Resident Governor of Timor reported that "several dozen to several hundred" dragons had been shot on Komodo, presumably during hunting expeditions for deer (Auffenberg, 1981).

Hunting regulations were authorized in 1940 outside of Java and Madura and they reinforced the governmental protection of the Komodo dragon. After his visit to the island in 1968, Dr. King reported that Sumbawa Islanders still occasionally poached deer on Komodo, although the government was trying to abolish the practice, which also encroached on the dragons' natural food supplies (King, 1968).

In 1970 the new reserve of Wai Wuul was established in western Flores, just south of Labuan Bajo. The
warden's office established in Reo in 1968 was moved to
Labuan Bajo in 1971. The Komodo National Park (Taman
Nasional Komodo) was established in 1980 but not dedicated by President Soeharto until 3 June 1988. A staff of
over 40 men and women are assigned to the park, divided
between the headquarters and tourist facilities on Komodo
itself, guardposts in Rinca and visitor centers in Labuan
Bajo and Sape (in Sumbawa).

It would appear that there has been some hunting
of dragons (both legal and illegal) over the years but not
to the extent of decimating the population. A number of
scientific groups from the 1926 Burden expedition to the
1962 Indonesian-Soviet expedition have found dragon
skeletons in traps set by the locals, though whether the
traps were to collect skins or simply to reduce the numbers of a feared predator is not known. Dr. Auffenberg
feels that both illegal zoo collecting and poaching may
still occur, even in recent years. In addition to the concern
that the wild population is depleted by these collections,
the herpetologist noted that, especially on Flores, if the
arrangement with the zoo falls through, or the Indonesian
trappers are afraid to transfer the dragon from the trap to
a cage, it is simply left in the trap to starve to death
(Auffenberg, 1981).

Another problem encountered on Flores is that
villagers sometimes illegally poison carrion bait with
insecticide to reduce the dragon population, like residents
of the American West poisoning sheep carcasses to rid
their ranches of coyotes and mountain lions. Dr.
Auffenberg reported that "it could become one of the
most difficult law enforcement problems in future ora
management" (Auffenberg, 1981).

Indonesia's changing political situation in the last

fifty years, along with all the other needs and problems of the emerging third world nation, have sometimes taken precedence over wildlife conservation. The Dutch East Indies were occupied by the Japanese during World War II, when a nominal self-government was established. Indonesia declared its independence on 17 August, 1945 and, after years of strife with the Dutch and then the British, was recognized as an independent nation in 1949. Like the United States, Indonesia dates its independence to the day it was declared, rather than to the end of the revolution. The nation suffered from a number of rebellions against its authoritarian leader, President Sukarno, who eventually was replaced by General Soeharto in 1966.

President Soeharto changed foreign and domestic policies to focus on economic rehabilitation and development, and since 1968 he has been re-elected four times to serve additional five-year terms. Despite some incidents of human rights violations and the taking of political prisoners, basic freedoms are respected, the standard of living is improving, and the economy is stable.

"The existence of a sound nature and wildlife conservation program in Indonesia is a good indication of the nation's progress and development," Dr. Auffenberg stated in his 1981 book.

Another human-created environmental problem for the dragons is competition from an introduced predator: feral dogs. The origin of these animals is principally deer poachers who bring them from other islands (usually Sumbawa) to assist in hunting, then fail to remove them. Domestic dogs kept by villagers have become less of a problem as national park regulations prohibiting them are more strictly enforced. Dr. Auffenberg (1981) expressed a strong concern that the deer population on Padar was being depleted by feral dogs and urged that they be exterminated so Komodo dragons could continue without competition for their prey. In fact, visits by park staff and international advisors in 1979-82 failed to document any further monitors on Padar, suggesting they have been locally exterminated (or simply have departed due to lack of food) (Robinson, 1991).

Some might question why the government allows people to continue to live in the dragon's range and thus subject themselves to the risk of being attacked. However, there is little evidence that local people within the Komodo dragon's range actually feel physically threatened. Snakebite is probably a much more common occurence, and few people would use this as rationale for departing a region their ancestors occupied for centuries.

Environmental Dangers

To date, the only captive-born dragons have been hatched in zoos in Java. Given that the wild population's total numbers are quite small, in the "worst-case scenario," if several disasters coincided, both the captive breeding population and the wild population could be destroyed. This concern fuels the Komodo Monitor Consortium's commitment to develop a second reproducing population of Komodo dragons elsewhere, for example in United States zoos.

A reproducing, captive colony would represent a hedge against the event of extinction of the wild populations. Our founder group would meet the needs of the world's zoos for exhibit stock. When managed and exhibited properly, this species is one of the highlights of the collection of any zoo (Bacon, et al, 1983).

Dr. King of the Bronx Zoo noted in 1970 that Komodo Island residents are gradually changing its environment, since each dry season they set sections of the waist-high grass on fire, either to (illegally) drive deer for hunting or to make it easier to gather fruit from the tamarind trees. The grass-seeds remain and the grass regrows, but many young trees are destroyed permanently through this process (King, 1970). Since 1982, when national park patrolling became more effective, the frequency of these fires has been reduced.

Dr. Auffenberg (1981) points out that, because of volcanic ash fall and lightning storms, the steppes and savannas of the dragons' range are periodically subject to fires and the dragons seem to be good at avoiding them, either by running or by retreating to their burrows. In the short term, however, fires hinder the dragons' hunting because they need tall grasses so they can sneak up on their prey. Permanent changes in the forested sections of the islands are also dangerous to the dragon and most other species, which rely on the shade provided by bushes and trees. John A. Phillips, comparative physiologist at the San Diego Zoo, told the *New York Times* of another potential danger from the annual human-caused fires: a major fire burning out of control in the savanna brush and grasses of Komodo could devastate the dragon species (Browne, 1986). Because savanna forest environments are perpetuated by naturally occurring fires, Dr. Auffenberg (1981) stated that plants, herbivores and dragons would benefit from controlled burns every four to six years when seasonal poacher-set fires have been eliminated.

Another environmental danger, pointed out by both Dr. Maruska and Johnny Arnett, is the possibility that, because Indonesia is part of the volcanic "ring of fire" around the edge of the Pacific Ocean, a Krakatoa-type eruption would threaten the future of the entire species.

Aside from the immediate destruction caused by the explosions, quakes, tornados, and possible tsunami waves, the most important aspect of volcanism in the Lesser Sundas is probably the ejection of large quantities of ash. In the great eruption at Krakatoa [in August of 1883], volcanic ash rose 40 km into the air and was dispersed around the world. Some floated for two years before it finally settled on the surface. ... Most of the approximately 44,000 people that perished as a result of the [1815] Tamboro eruption [on Lombok Island]did so because of the heavy ash fall (Auffenberg, 1981).

Adult Komodo dragons actually benefited from a Flores volcano eruption in 1969; falling ash killed plant life and clogged waterholes, so the herbivore species were weakened and easy to kill (Auffenberg, 1981). In the case of more sustained ash fall, however, the whole ecology of the dragons' range could be affected. Permanent reduction in prey populations would cause severe problems for the predator dragons as well.

This study shows that both the number of oras and the area they inhabit are larger than supposed and that extinction is not imminent. But the geographic range of the ora is small, and history has shown that animals so situated are highly vulnerable. Therefore, vigilance and a policy of conservation and enforcement are necessary (Auffenberg, 1981).

According to David Quammen, island species, due to their long isolation from the larger ecosystem, almost invariably become extinct "without ever rejoining the mainstream of evolution" (Quammen, 1986). Both dragons and tuataras ended up with highly specialized adaptations that made them unable to continue evolving and adapt to new environments. It cannot be denied that Komodo dragons are evolutionarily limited to islands they no longer find to be trouble-free paradises; like the tuataras, they are "extremely specialized forms hanging on to existence by the thinnest margin" (Savage, 1963). Humans, the new and highly intrusive primary consumer, have the powerful capability to hurry an island species to premature extinction, as it did with dodos. Conservationists may not be able to interfere with the eventual natural extinction of the Komodo dragon in the far-distant future, but they believe people have an obligation to protect the vulnerable species in the present.

7

CONSERVATIONISTS' HOPES FOR THE FUTURE

Imagine joining a typical young family — two parents and three children — on their way to the zoo in the early 1960's. It is a small, rather poor zoo, so the children can guess what their favorite exhibits will be before they even enter the gate: the lion, the bear, and the panther. One child clamors for cotton candy immediately, another wants to get an inflatable toy animal, and the third stares fixedly at two crocodiles and a handful of flamingos sharing a space-saving outdoor exhibit. A badger paces ceaselessly around the concrete floor of its small cage. The children find the monkeys a bit livelier, though the cages are also bare and exposed to the elements in the summer. The adult reader will probably recall a similar zoo from childhood — perhaps larger and wealthier, but still working to sell entertainment to the public at the smallest possible overhead cost.

Today, zoos attempt to duplicate the specimens' original environment as much as possible, providing much more humane exhibits. The focus, too, has changed to educating the public about species conservation and, with financial assistance from corporate underwriters and the general public, developing breeding and exchange programs. In the past, zoos with conservationist interests did not receive much popular support — what was the logic in attempting to maintain a species that did not provide a direct benefit to humanity? An example in the United States is the passenger pigeon: in pioneer days, numerous flocks decimated crops across North America so farmers and hunters considered the species no better than pests — an endless source of recreational shooting and food. During the first decade of the twentieth century, the Cincinnati Zoo and Botanical Garden offered a reward for anyone able to provide a mate for the aging Martha, the last passenger pigeon in captivity. Once, a farm boy shot an unusual bird, slender and long-tailed, which he found among the wild birds in the yard; the dead bird proved to be the last known wild passenger pigeon. The final hope of her species, Martha died in 1914. (Cincinnati Zoo, Passenger Pigeon Memorial)

Although the passenger pigeons once flew in flocks so huge they darkened the sky overhead, the little-known Komodo dragon, which apparently never numbered much more than about 5,000 adults at one time, has been collected and killed because of its rarity. Unlike passenger pigeons, hunted to extinction as pests, Komodo dragons have been gathered primarily in the name of science, to provide specimens for museum and zoo collections. The Griswold-Harkness expedition in 1934 captured 43 dragons apparently for sport, since the Americans were only allowed to remove eight dragons from the island. The Indonesian-Soviet expedition of 1962 killed and dissected three dragons on Komodo itself in order to learn more about the species' reproductive systems. In addition, as explained in the previous chapter, poachers and trappers at first had little fear of being caught in the nearly inaccessible ranges of the dragon, regardless of the legal protection given by native and colonial law.

Despite the lesson of the passenger pigeons, reptiles — especially the larger, uglier, and more dangerous species — had even less likelihood than birds of receiving human protection in the early part of the twentieth century. As recently as 1965, the Kenyan government allowed Alistaire Graham and Peter Beard, former game department employees, to study Lake Rudolph crocodiles, funding their work by selling the skins of the dead animals. In his book about the project, Alistaire Graham justified killing 500 members of the species, which had just been upgraded from vermin to game, by stating that the crocodiles had to be studied to determine whether they were worth preserving (Graham, 1973). It must be noted that the gruesome photograph of still recognizable human legs pulled from the belly of a just-killed crocodile helps support the author's point.

Environmental Success Story

In the 80-odd years since the human world officially discovered Komodo dragons, they have been stuffed and displayed in museums and even in a bar, mistaken for dinosaurs or crocodiles, shipped to cold foreign lands and displayed in cement-floored zoo cages, and described as cannibalistic, man-eating monsters, but still the species has survived without apparent depletion in its native islands. This environmental success story is a continuing process, however, and herpetologists, zoo conservationists, and the Indonesian government all propose different methods of continuing to protect the species from extinction.

Dr. Auffenberg, commissioned to suggest a management program for the species, recommended limiting the Komodo Island feedings to once a week, protecting the dragons' natural environment, and balancing the numbers of those removed for zoo collections to maintain the range's natural ratio of 3.5 males to 1 female. Zoo representatives, at least those in the United States, have a different ambition — to establish a captive population of breeding dragons so zoo collections will not undermine the ecological balance of dragons in their native setting. As noted in Chapter 6, zoological societies also hope that building a captive reproducing population will provide a safeguard against extinction, in case the native population is destroyed by catastrophe. Indonesia itself attempts to reconcile the many aspects of the Komodo dragon as tourist attraction, natural resource, and goal of many zoo collectors.

Dr. Auffenberg's Recommendations

"The preservation of the ora should be accepted as one of the highest priorities in conservation of the world's reptiles," Dr. Auffenberg (1981) concluded after his field study of the Komodo dragon.

According to the '1988 IUCN Red Book List of Threatened Animals' prepared by the World Conservation Monitoring Centre, the species [Komodo monitor] is assigned a category of 'RARE' which represents the following: Taxa [groups in a scientific classification] with small world populations that are not at present 'Endangered' or 'Vulnerable', but are at risk. These taxa are usually localized within restricted geographical areas or habitats or are thinly scattered over a more extensive range (Kaneko, 1990).

Although not officially an endangered species, the dragon

is an island-dweller, unable to adapt to sudden change; its existence may be threatened by over-zealous zoo collecting, the inevitable increase in tourism, or environmental changes caused by humans. Although he felt the Rinca and Komodo populations were well protected, Dr. Auffenberg worried that the small reserve of Wai Wuul would not save a large enough population of the Flores dragons and suggested that an additional reserve be established along the north coast near Pota (Auffenberg, 1981). Although a Pota reserve has not been implemented, there now exists a second Flores reserve, at Mbeliling Nggorang on the west coast (Robinson, 1991).

> The clear predominance of male specimens in the island population of monitors apparently is no accident, but rather reflects the actual ratio of sexes existing in nature. It is possible that the sharp reduction in number of females is the manifestation of a special mechanism of regulation of the number which prevents overpopulation of the monitors on the island Komodo. The small territory of the island, together with the limited amount of food (carrion),... might fully play the role of factors that have produced in the process of evolution the selection of such a mechanism (Darevskii and Kadarsan, 1964).

Auffenberg (1981) corroborated the Indonesian-Soviet expedition's report quoted above on the high ratio of males, both in the wild and in zoo and museum collections. He recommended that, in order to help maintain the gender balance in the wild, for every four males taken from the wild, only one female dragon should be removed. Also, he advised that only monitors 3 feet, 3 inches to 5 feet (1 to 1.5 m) be captured for zoos. The larger animals may be desired by zoos but they are relatively scarce and needed to maintain reproduction in the wild. Since medium-sized dragons in the wild have a high mortality rate due to starvation, disease or fights with larger dragons, taking dragons in that size class for zoos will save a number of individuals that would otherwise have died before reproducing. The natural population size will be maintained in the wild, and with patience and time a reproducing zoo population can be built.

The harvesting of live specimens for zoos appears to be successfully controlled by present government regulations and the input of the International Union for the Conservation of Nature and Natural Resources. In 1956, the Indonesian government began limiting dragon collectors from foreign zoos to a total of 12 monitors every three years. (King, 1968) Since at least 1964, when a pair of dragons were given to the National Zoo in Washington, D.C., as an emblem of international goodwill, the Komodo monitors have been treated as a national treasure which cannot leave the country except as a gift from the Indonesian government. This tight control is further justified since Indonesia is a signatory to the Convention on International Trade in Endangered Species of Wild Fauna and Flora which severely limits export of formally listed animals even for research and display. Museums and scientists interested in obtaining specimens for stuffing or anatomical study must now wait until zoo dragons die. Indonesia has also begun capturing dragons while they are very young and raising them in the Ragunan or Surabaya zoo. When the president offers dragons as a gift to another country, a pair are chosen from the existing zoo populations rather than being removed from the wild.

As noted in Chapter 6, human children, the elderly, and the sick are in the most danger from dragons on Komodo and Flores. Dr. Auffenberg (1981) suggested that government zoo collecting policy take that fact into consideration in Komodo's case, since the number of attacks might increase in frequency as the number of tourists grows.

> Though the legal 'harvest' of oras [Komodo
> dragons] of small size on Komodo and Rintja
> [Rinca] could probably be doubled without dam-
> age to population levels, the capture of oras on
> Padar and Flores should be completely prohib-
> ited at present. Population densities on these
> islands are too low to allow any captures
> (Auffenberg, 1981).

Most of the recent attack stories come from Flores, as do all rumors of dragons dying from poisoned bait, and the dragon population on Flores may be the largest of any one of the four islands in the dragons' permanent range. As a result, Indonesian zoo representatives now concentrate their collection efforts on Flores where the interaction between humans and dragons is more stressful and removing young dragons may reduce future ten- sions between the two species. No effort is made to encourage tourists to visit the Komodo monitor reserves on Flores.

On Komodo Island, however, the growing number of tourists increases the likelihood that a nega- tive encounter between dragons and tourists will occur. In a 1986 interview, Dr. Phillips reported that some tourists at the feeding arena were foolhardy enough to feed goat meat to the dragons by hand (Browne, 1986). No other references have been found of people hand- feeding dragons in the wild, so it is to be hoped that Dr. Phillips observed an isolated incident that the rangers now take measures to prevent. Another unwise activity, as Dick Lutz learned personally, is moving among any group of monitors at the feeding arena, whether or not there is bait being offered.

Two defenses can be recommended to minimize the chance of attacks on tourists: adequate training and numbers of rangers, who also serve as guides to all planned contacts between tourists and dragons on Komodo Island, and education of tourists before they arrive at Komodo National Park. Tourists must be aware they are entering the range of potentially dangerous wild animals and should act accordingly.

The presence of a settled village and such aspects of civilization as beer and toilets can mislead tourists into assuming that the visit to Komodo Island is no more dangerous than, for example, an overnight campout in a park near home. The wooden jetty, neatly laid out path, and visitors' compound (complete with administration center, cafeteria and museum) all combined "to diminish our sense of intrepidness" (Adams and Carwardine, 1990). The authors soon discovered, however, that the apparently stuffed four-foot-long (1.2) dragon in the middle of the road was not only alive but also about to successfully attack the chickens planned for supper. A reader intending to visit Komodo National Park should treat the trip as seriously as a safari into lion country, reading available literature first and taking necessary precautions. These include wearing long pants and boots to protect against snake bite, remaining near the visitors' compound unless accompanied by a guide, and never leaving the group during hikes around the island. It is strongly advised that children, the elderly and anyone in poor health choose a safer vacation; the long boat ride and extreme heat during the tourist season are sufficient reason, along with the dragons, for all potential visitors to Komodo Island to evaluate their health and endurance before deciding to make the trip.

Dr. Auffenberg (1981) recommended that the

number of feedings per month be limited and that the location of the feeding be varied. Although the dragons are still fed in a single location, since January 1989 they are now fed only once a week, on Sundays, and the national park uses ranger-guides to protect the dragons from poachers and the visitors from the dragons. When Dick and Mary Lutz visited Rinca, for instance, they were the only visitors and there were seven ranger-guides.

The Zoo Tomorrow

"A zoo is not just a custodian of individual animals," Dr. Philips of the San Diego Zoo told a *New York Times* interviewer (Brown, 1986). "A zoo has a duty to help animals breed and keep the species going."

In 1981, curators from zoos in San Diego, New York, Philadelphia, and Florida founded the Komodo Monitor Consortium with the goal of obtaining a minimum of 15 unrelated juvenile dragons to establish a zoo population of breeding animals. Space availability, specimen compatibility, breeding success, and exhibition needs would determine which animals were settled in which zoos. Ideally, a second generation of dragons would be hatched, and genetic considerations would also be a consideration in the distribution of the individuals.

Due to its limited range and relatively small population, the Komodo monitor is protected by the Republic of Indonesia, CITES [Convention on the International Trade of Endangered Species], and the USDI [United States Department of the Interior]. Any serious perturbation could have disastrous consequences. A reproducing, captive colony would represent a hedge against the event of extinction of the wild populations (Bacon et al, 1983).

Since its establishment, the KMC has grown to include a number of zoos, including those in Washington, D.C., and Cincinnati, which each received a pair of dragons in 1988 and 1990 respectively. At the present writing, negotiations are in progress over the possibility of a third pair of dragons being donated to the United States for inclusion in the San Diego Zoo collection. Both the National Zoo and the San Diego Zoo have kept dragons in the past, while the Cincinnati Zoo is well-known for its conservationist programs with other species. Although unfamiliar with the consortium at the time it received the dragons, the Cincinnati Zoo has since then been accepted as a member of the group.

"Not one single zoo can accomplish this — it has to be a network of zoos," said Dr. Maruska, director of the Cincinnati Zoo, in a December 1990 interview. He hopes that once a breeding population of dragons in several United States zoos has been established, the American Association of Zoos, Parks and Aquariums will add the Komodo dragon to its Species Survival Plan. Over 50 species are now managed through the SSP to increase their zoo populations without draining resources in the wild. One zoo is named to coordinate the pooled efforts of all participating zoos, Dr. Maruska explained, and they are thus able to exchange offspring and improve husbandry of the species (Maruska, 1990).

Indonesia is already in part fulfilling the goals of the Komodo Monitor Consortium by raising captive-bred dragons for other zoos. However, the KMC would like to see the breeding dragon population spread across at least 15 zoos to preserve a varied gene pool. Since the KMC is a group of American zoos, the members would like the participating zoos to be based in the United States. However, the location of these breeding populations could also be European, Asian, or African zoos. (In addition, by collecting young dragons from the wild and raising them, as well as captive-born populations, in zoo enclosures, Indonesia is helping to fulfill several other stipulations of Dr. Auffenberg.) Whether the yearlings caught in the wild are sexed at the time of their capture is unknown, but at any rate this approach does not reduce the existing population of breeding adults. Furthermore, zoo collectors continue to request mated pairs so they can attempt captive reproduction. By choosing primarily from their captive and captive-born collection, the Indonesian zoos will not have to worry about upsetting the male-female ratio of dragons in the wild.

"If you take off a few, it's wise harvesting, essentially, as long as it's done under biological controls," explained Dr. Maruska. He said the IUCN feels that the wild dragon population is stable enough to allow the export of up to five dragons a year. Dr. Auffenberg's ideal ratio of four male dragons for every female may not be achieved, partially because sexing the dragons is so difficult and partially because zoos prefer to acquire reproductive pairs. However, the goals of naturalists and zoo curators are not necessarily at odds, because the intent of zoo curators is to eventually develop a captive breeding population so the remaining wild dragons may flourish undisturbed by collectors. For example, Dr. Maruska said the Cincinnati Zoo chose two of the smaller dragons from among the animals available at the Ragunan Zoo because they were a healthy young pair which had already been observed in mating behavior. Larger animals might not adapt to the new environment as well, he noted, adding that the zoological society hopes the dragons, estimated to be in the range of 7 to 10 years old, will have a long reproductive life (Maruska, 1990).

Another possibility of establishing captive breeding programs was introduced in 1986 by Dr. Phillips, at the San Diego Zoo. At the time, the zoo's male dragon had recently died, and the zoo's surviving female dragon,

Sunshine, was the only Komodo dragon in captivity in the United States.

Dr. Phillips and his colleagues believe that the female can be stimulated to ovulate by administration of a substance called gonadotropin releasing hormone, which is commercially derived from chickens. The hormone must be administered continuously for about two weeks to induce ovulation.

When the attempt to impregnate the female Komodo dragon begins later this year [1986], a capsule containing the hormone will be implanted under a flap of her skin. Inside the capsule is a pump powered by the osmotic pressure of the animal's own fluids to release the hormone a little at a time. When ovulation begins, impregnation by semen from the deceased male dragon [which had been extracted and preserved in liquid nitrogen] will be attempted (Brown, 1986).

Although the attempt to impregnate the 18-year-old Sunshine ultimately failed, the implanted hormone pump method developed by Dr. Phillips and his colleague William Lasley of University of California Davis was successfully used to increase the green iguana population of Belize. Dr. Phillips noted that human intervention in endangered species reproduction is "only a last-ditch measure" but it should be part of the "survival arsenal" available to conservationists.

"If you wait too long to try to save a species, you may find that too few animals are left to make a comeback," he concluded. "I hope that the imminent passing of the California condor has taught all of us a lesson" (Brown, 1986).

Here There Be Dragons

"For the future, as long as there remains an adequate supply of game and the animals are left alone, there should be no danger of extinction," noted Marvin Jones (1964). However, he was writing in the days before tourists began regularly visiting Komodo Island in 1969, partially in response to the 1968 *National Geographic* article by James Kern, which further publicized the little-known Komodo dragon to the world. The feeding ritual — which combines elements of the fascinating, educational, and disgusting — enables tourists to observe Komodo dragons relatively easily and will undoubtedly continue. According to the World Conservation Union, the Komodo dragon population is stable and unlikely to become endangered unless over-tourism creates a threat to the species (Edwards, 1990).

The Indonesian government feels an obligation to its impoverished nation to make the dragons accessible to tourists, ideally as a sustainable resource. The question is similar to that faced in over-popular national parks in the United States: how can the Yosemite National Park staff, for instance, maintain a beautiful wilderness site while still keeping the gates open to all visitors, no matter how many there may be. With Komodo Island, the problem, at least for now, is not how large to build the tourists' quarters or how often to schedule the ferries from Labuan Bajo and Bima, but rather how much to limit tourists' access to the dragons.

"Indonesia is a model of a successful developing nation....[but] still one of the poorest nations in southeast Asia," reports Bill Dalton in *Indonesia Handbook* (Dalton, 1988). The Indonesians rightfully consider the Komodo dragon to be a national treasure, not only for its own sake but also as a tourist attraction. The nearly undeveloped region of the Lesser Sunda Islands has no big name appeal and lush green environment, such as Bali uses to attract the tourist trade. Komodo National Park was established in 1980, but more recently it has received such official touches as the 1988 park dedication by President Soeharto and the souvenirs for sale at the Labuan Bajo ranger station.

Bela Demeter of the National Zoo in Washington, D.C., visited Komodo in 1988, before the one-goat-per-week limit was established. He identified a concern of many naturalists — how to maintain a balance between tourists' right to view the dragons and the growing commercialism which he feared might lead to domestication.

> Three thousand groups [of tourists] each year is a significant number; will increasing numbers lead to increased commercialism and development? How many more feeding arenas can be created before Komodo's remaining groups of lizards in fact become domesticated? And yet, it is the attention of tourists and their economic clout that makes these animals a resource worth conserving in the eyes of some of the country's decision-makers.
>
> To balance the beneficial and negative aspects of the tourist trade, the Indonesians have designated an area of Komodo Island as a sanctuary zone where tourism is prohibited. ...Having witnessed the remarkable spectacle of the dragons first-hand, we can only be encouraged by Indonesia's efforts to promote wildlife tourism while offsetting its impact on the dragons' lifestyle. (Demeter, 1988)

Ecotourism

The Galapagos Islands may provide a valuable lesson in island ecology and management to those interested in the future of the Komodo dragon. In both cases, the responsibility for protecting an ecological wonder has fallen to a relatively poor undeveloped country. The battle to preserve the Galapagos appeared to have been won in 1959 when Ecuador declared most of the area a national park and the Darwin Foundation was chartered to help protect the islands made famous by Charles Darwin. The Foundation's Darwin Station has engaged in captive breeding programs, including 800 giant tortoises and several land iguana species, according to the 1986 Discovery Channel film "Galapagos". (Plage, 1986)

Organized tourism began in 1969 and interest has grown dramatically since then, according to Alan C. Miller in his 1990 newspaper article, "New Popularity Proves Harmful to Galapagos." About 50,000 tourists were expected to visit the island in 1990, more than twice the number of visitors five years earlier. Authorities are presently building a third airstrip, and politically well-connected entrepreneurs have sought to build luxury resorts. The permanent human population increased from about 6,000 to 14,000 in eight years and continues to grow at the rate of 12 percent a year. Former fishing villages feature a growing number of souvenir shops, restaurants, and discos, yet the budget for the national park was severely cut in the 1980's, reducing the number of park rangers (Miller, 1990).

In the Galapagos, formerly unoccupied by any mammal species, predators introduced by humans have proliferated. Rats attack penguin chicks and tortoise eggs and hatchlings; feral dogs and cats threaten the land iguana populations and baby penguins; and feral pigs dig up and eat green sea turtle eggs. Feral goats —

introduced to provide meat for the human population —
have eliminated much of the native vegetation on some
islands, replacing the giant tortoises in the large herbivore niche. Beginning in 1982, naturalists at the Darwin
Station have dug up the wild-laid eggs of endangered
iguana species to hatch them in greater safety. Before
releasing the captive-raised iguanas and tortoises, station
personnel try to rid the islands of the feral goats, dogs and
cats that pose a danger to the native wildlife reintroduced
into the environment. Similarly, in order to give petrel
eggs a chance to survive, hundreds of rat traps were set
daily over a three-year period on one island (Plage, 1986).

The film reported that tourist numbers are limited to 25,000 a year but there are constant pressures to
raise that figure because the island reserve needs tourist
dollars to survive. Although the concern about human
impact is belated, the number of tourists at any one time
is limited, and each cruise ship stopping at the Galapagos
is required to have a trained guide to accompany the
tourists onshore (Plage, 1986).

> Today the Galapagos Islands are an Ecuador-
> ian national park, with strict regulations pro-
> tecting the native wildlife and vegetation from
> being tampered with by the likes of you or
> me. Even Darwin himself would now need a
> research permit. ...The Galapagos require ex-
> traordinary, uncompromised protection from
> human impact. ...because they have already,
> in the past three hundred years, been pillaged
> almost beyond rescue...because they hold
> precious significance in our natural and our
> intellectual heritage...because they now en-
> dure heavy traffic as a tourist destination.
> (Quammen, 1988)

Like most developing regions, Indonesia encourages foreign tourism as one way to augment its economy and help give its people a better life. In all likelihood, Indonesia can also expect a dramatic increase in tourism to the homeland of the Komodo dragon: the annual number of tourists at present is small compared to the number that may arrive in the future, but Komodo National Park restrictions were designed to control the expected increase in visitors. The few tourists that make the difficult trip to see the Komodo dragon are obviously hardy souls who are interested in the experience. To use one of the new words of the late twentieth century, they are ecotourists.

Environmentally sensitive tour operators and government officials joined environmentalists at the 28-nation International Symposium for Ecotourism held in Miami in late 1990, reported Associate Press writer Beth Duff-Brown. She learned that ecotourists concentrate on understanding the culture and environment they are visiting rather than impinging on the natural resources they are enjoying. Furthermore, their interest and money help to ensure the preservation of precious natural resources and endangered species.

An ecologically responsible tour group is Voyagers International, P.O. Box 915, Ithaca, NY, 14851. They can be reached by telephone at (607) 257-3091. Boyd Norton, the photographer who took the photograph on this book's cover periodically leads photographic tours to Komodo for Voyagers International.

"The only person who is interested in preservation of the wildlife and the national parks is the quality visitor," said Kailash Sankhala, president and founder of Tiger Trust of India. "He's the only friend the national park has left."

...Sankhala was a government forester for 35 years, before becoming interested in saving the tiger in India. In 1972, there were only 1,827 tigers left. Today, there are 4,300 tigers on 18 reserves in India, paid for in great part with tourist dollars. (Duff-Brown, 1991)

Another example of ecotourism's beneficial effects concerns the Rwanda mountain gorillas made famous by zoologist Dian Fossey. Concerned about the conversion of part of Volcano National Park into cattle grazing land, environmentalists persuaded government officials to leave the range of the endangered species untouched except for money-earning guided hiking tours. Over $1,000,000 is grossed annually from the 5,000 to 6,000 tourists who visit the gorillas in the wild, and with the preservation of their range, the number of gorillas has increased from 275 in the early 1970's to more than 400. (Duff-Brown, 1991)

Future of Komodo National Park

According to Alan Robinson, a technical advisor to Indonesia's park system (PHPA) who first began assisting development at Komodo National Park in 1970, and whose most recent inspection was in late 1990, there has been a mixture of progress and problems since earlier visitors have made their reports.

On the positive side, an increasingly professional and dedicated staff of rangers and administrators permanently reside on Komodo at the village and the headquarters visitor complex, with rotating shifts of patrol rangers at Loh Buaya and Rinca village on Rinca. A radio system operates at least periodically and routine patrols, in conjunction with armed provincial police, have had a significant impact in reducing deer poaching and illegal burning.

A 1978 park management plan is being implemented. Most significantly, the plan's zoning concept is in force, with about 90 percent of Komodo and nearly all of Rinca in either a strict no entry sanctuary status or with-guide-only primitive wilderness status. No roads, motorized vehicles or permanent airstrips have been permitted on either island. Nearly all of the park's visitors (estimated at 10,000-15,000 for 1991) are led by guides only to one location within the ten percent of Komodo open to "intensive use," i.e. the visitor complex and dragon feeding arena. Most of the visitors stay overnight at the tourist cottages provided by the park though some stay on board the small charter boats on which they arrive. Ten or more groups per year arrive on rather luxurious 100 to 150 passenger cruise ships.

On the negative side, Alan Robinson reports that operating budgets remain low and equipment and frequency of patrols needs to be improved to establish permanent control over the major poaching and fishing problems. Village populations have grown, especially on Komodo. Local villagers, who are exclusively fishermen, have little direct impact on Komodo dragons, but increasing human populations may eventually demand larger residential areas and compete for scarce water resources. Politics, government controls, taxation and schooling all become more complicated as the population grows, requiring greater and greater conflict-resolution skills on the part of the park staff. Research on Komodo monitors, including census taking and population estimating, has not been conducted very aggressively or extensively (despite provision of a field laboratory at the headquarters site). Little recent documented study has occured which would aid park staff in setting strategies for managing dragon habitat, especially as better and better control over poaching and burning is established. It is encouraging to learn a long-term study with resident foreign and Indonesian scientists will begin in 1991 to address gaps in natural history information and reexamine Dr. Auffenberg's population estimates.

According to Alan Robinson, the park still has difficulty in balancing visitors' desire to see Komodo monitors with the need to provide a safe experience for visitors and avoid interfering in the behavior of most dragons. He worries that extensive interference could affect species survival.

Alan Robinson is reasonably confident that species survival will not be affected by the present practice of weekly feeding in a single location in the one intensive use zone, which involves perhaps 30 individual animals (about 1 percent of the adult Komodo Island dragon population). Alan Robinson reports that it has long been officially prohibited to allow visitors inside the feeding area regardless of whether or not the rangers feel they can control aggressive behavior. Individual tourists or non-park group guides tend to pressure park rangers to allow special access to the dragons, such as manipulating the bait. Direct interspecies contact at feeding time can be extremely dangerous to humans, he feels.

The American ranger reports that the park's primary goal is to deemphasize the feeding arena experience and encourage a deeper exploration of both monitor and island ecology through longer, even overnight, guided hikes and exploration. Perhaps few monitors will actually be seen, but their tracks and signs and those of their food species are easily interpreted into an exciting and educational story. Spectacular views of the islands, meetings with villagers, even traditional fishing expeditions and snorkeling and scuba diving are easily arranged. These more extensive visits would require a two or three day stay and some expenditure of energy by reasonably fit and motivated visitors. Alan Robinson concludes that this plan would require knowledgeable park rangers (or park-trained and certified guides) with foreign language skills (Robinson, 1991).

If the habitat of the Komodo dragon is not to suffer the fate of the Galapagos Islands, environmentalists of the world and the government of Indonesia must maintain continued vigilance as the number of tourists to the area escalates. With environmentalists' help, Indonesia's enlightened and helpful policy will preserve the Komodo dragon species and make it possible for many people to observe the reptile in the wild without destroying its habitat or reducing its population.

APPENDIX : The Trip to Komodo Island

Arriving at the pier on Komodo Island

If it were superimposed on North America, the country of Indonesia would stretch from California to Bermuda; including the water between the islands, Indonesia's total area is larger than that of the United States. The total land area, though, is only about 735,381 square miles (1,176,610 square km)— unequally divided among 13,677 islands — of which only 6,044 are named and 922 inhabited. The 1989 census figures show 187,726,000 Indonesians, making it the fifth-largest country in the world in terms of population, just behind the United States, whose 247,100,000 residents give it the fourth largest national population ranking. In all this vast region, Komodo dragons are native to seven south eastern Indonesian islands, of which only Flores is large enough to appear on a global map. Indonesia's economic resources include coal mines, oil fields, and plantations (rubber, tobacco, coffee, tea, etc.), but the people of the Greater and Lesser Sunda Islands primarily raise rice and corn. The eastern islands are still an impoverished outpost compared to modern cities such as Jakarta, so it is no surprise that the government has seen the value of Komodo dragons in drawing tourists to the Sunda Islands.

Indonesia has been called a girdle of emeralds strung around the equator, and green predominates in the Indonesian landscape, the sombre green of tropical rain forests, the varied greens of coconut palm and banana plant, the brilliant green of young rice in the terraced rice fields (Zainu'ddin, 1970).

Indonesia's weather is limited to two seasons: rainy and dry. Bali and other western Indonesian islands have a long rainy season and are indeed tropical paradises. On the other side of Wallace's line, though, the islands are extremely hot and dry for most of the year. Earthquakes and volcanic eruptions are frequent in Indonesia, and the Lesser Sunda Islands, with active volcanos on Sumbawa and Flores, are no exception. Ash falls throughout the region, sometimes months or even years after a volcano has erupted.

Komodo Island is the main and best-known habitat of the Komodo dragon. Dr. Auffenberg's 1969/70 census estimated that perhaps 3,000 monitors live on the island, though a 1985/86 World Wildlife Fund survey reportedly counted only 1,674. The two figures' variance may represent a decrease in overall population, but perhaps it indicates that Dr. Auffenberg estimated the total based on the population density of those he was able to evaluate, while the later survey counted as many individuals as could be identified. The dry, mountainous island covers 94.5 square miles (about 245 square km) and is mostly high grassy plains dotted with scattered trees. Other than the savanna, about 30 percent of the island is thickly forested with trees that flourish during each year's brief rainy season. Komodo is uninhabited by humans except for the ranger station and Kampung Komodo, the small village whose population swells during the fishing season to approximately 700. According to the text of a Cincinnati Zoo slide presentation on Komodo National Park, the island will not hold a large permanent human population due to the shortage of fresh water. ("Text: Komodo National Park", 1990) A single permanent well exists near Kampung Komodo.

The World Wildlife Fund survey counted 1,128 dragons on Rinca, the large island between Komodo and Flores, where the human population is limited to the ranger station at Loh Buaya and Rinca village, the only permanent settlement on the island. There is no ferry to Rinca, but it is possible to hire a boat to visit there.

There are no human inhabitants of Padar, which Douglas Burden (1928) described as "for the most part an arid, upraised coral reef": he felt it was probably not an ideal environment for the Komodo dragon, which seems to survive best where there is a combination of dry hot lands and thick jungle. This observation may explain why the number of dragons on Padar has apparently always been small, while the dragons do well on wetter Flores, with its mangrove swamps. Dr. Auffenberg visited the island for two short trips during his year-long study of the dragons. At the time, he estimated that only a few dozen dragons lived on Padar. In recent years, only occasional tracks and fecal remains on the beach have indicated the dragons' continued existence there, and some herpetologists believe that the always elusive dragons of Padar may have died off entirely (Strimple, 1990). According to Dr. Auffenberg (1981), dragons definitely inhabit the small island of Gili Mota and may be either residents or transient visitors on tiny Oewada Sami. As detailed in Chapter 3, dragons do not live on Nusa Mbarapu just off Komodo but merely swim over occasionally to feast on wild game and the goats pastured there by the natives of nearby islands.

Komodo monitors are also found in a number of coastal locations in the extreme western region of Flores. One concentration of dragons just across the narrow strait from Rinca is called Wai Wuul, where several thousand acres are now in a reserve administered by Komodo National Park. Perhaps several hundred Komodo dragons live there.

Although Flores as a whole supports perhaps 1,000,000 human inhabitants, the western province is still sparsely populated. This may explain why Komodo monitors have persisted in these small pockets despite pressure from humans, who tend to hunt the lizards to protect their domestic animals.

"I have never known a more salubrious [healthy] spot to live and work in," commented Douglas Burden (1928), describing his four weeks on Komodo Island in the summer of 1926. Lyall Watson (1987), who visited in both 1965 and 1986, called it one of the most beautiful places on earth.

Visitors' responses to Komodo Island, however, are as different as the people themselves and even those who consider the island a paradise realize the loveliness is counterbalanced by the presence of some animal species which can be dangerous. As James Kern noted, some of the fauna are "not as docile as the dragons"; the less enjoyable (but not hazardous) animals he encountered during his two weeks camped out on Komodo Island included cave bats, large hairy hunting spiders, and land crabs. He also had close encounters with a cobra and a green viper and worried that his swims in the bay might culminate in a meeting with a shark or sea snake (Kern, 1968).

Douglas Adams, a more recent visitor who stayed within the official tourist range, was bothered by what he called the island's "strong, thick, musty smell" and found the combination of rats and spiders in the tourists' quarters drove him to sleep on the deck of the boat instead. He also felt the chicken-eating dragon he first encountered was an arrogant murderer, though he admitted he was reading evil intent into the dragon's natural hunting instinct.

> Whatever malign emotions we tried to pin on to the lizard, we knew that they weren't the lizard's emotions at all, only ours. The lizard was simply going about its lizardly business in a simple, straightforward lizardly way (Adams and Carwardine, 1990).

"Unlike any other part of the world except India, [Komodo] is cursed with all four classes of poisonous snakes," Douglas Burden admitted in his 1928 book. By the time of Adams' and Carwardine's visit in the late 1980's, the types of snakes and other poisonous animals had been more thoroughly identified. Venom specialist Struan Sutherland told the two men that fifteen snake species live on Komodo, of which about half are poisonous. He added that only the Russell's viper, the bamboo viper, and the Indian cobra are capable of killing humans with their venom. Dr. Sutherland also warned of dangers offshore: scorpion fish, stone fish, and sea snakes that he said are much more poisonous than any land animals (Adams and Carwardine, 1990).

The methods of visiting Komodo Island are almost as varied as people's reactions to the place, but no route, other than the red carpet helicopter ride provided for President Soeharto in 1988, is terribly easy. For their 1968 trip, before tourist routes had been established, Dr. King, James Kern, and their party chartered a 45-foot-long, wooden-hulled freighter to sail the 500 miles from Surabaya, Java to Komodo Island in three days. One and a half days into the trip, the engine's drive shaft broke, setting them adrift for five anxious hours until a passing military boat pulled the trawler into Buleleng, Bali. They waited a week until another ship came along. The delay meant that the scientists were only able to stay on Komodo for two days, but James Kern, the expedition photographer, remained behind for another two weeks, since his schedule allowed him to wait for the next trawler to arrive (Kern, 1968; King, 1968).

Since 1973, cruise ships have occasionally included Komodo Island on their itinerary, standing offshore while smaller boats bring people and their luggage to shore.

One tour package in a 1987 pamphlet, for example, described a six-day trip beginning and ending in Bali and including stops on Flores, Komodo Island and Sumbawa. More frequently, visitors fly in to Flores from Java or Bali, taking Merpati Air, a commuter airline. There are several ways to arrange the details of an air and ocean voyage to Komodo, but all of them are subject to change, as a travel agency director explained to one group of visitors after their confirmed plane tickets from Denpasar Airport on Bali were refused and they missed the plane.

> He explained that if you are traveling in Indonesia you should allow four or five days for any thing urgent to happen. As far as our missing plane seats were concerned, he said that this sort of thing happened all the time. Often some government official or other important person would decide that he needed a seat, and, of

course, someone else would then lose theirs. We asked if this was what happened to us. He said, no, it wasn't the reason, but it was the sort of reason we should bear in mind when thinking about these problems (Adams and Carwardine, 1990).

Tourists who choose the air route usually take a series of short flights from Bali to Lombok to Sumbawa and finally fly over Komodo Island to land in Labuan Bajo on Flores. From there, it is only a three to five hour boat ride to Komodo. Several other routes exist, but are less frequently used because they require a long drive across Flores to Labuan Bajo or a 10-hour boat journey from Sape, on Sumbawa. Although tourists need permits to visit Komodo National Park, these can be acquired in Labuan Bajo or Sape, rather like buying a pass at the entrance to a national park in the United States.

Less adventurous tourists can sign up for a pre-arranged tour, which does not include an actual tour guide: the tourist is met at the airport in Labuan Bajo, taken to pre-arranged accommodations, and placed on a pre-reserved boat for Komodo. This certainly takes much of the sweat and worry out of the trip but also removes some of the adventure and flexibility. Bela Demeter, from the National Zoo in Washington, D.C., had a perhaps more typical "roughing it" journey in 1988, over much the same route that Dick and Mary Lutz took on their 1989 trip.

> As luck would have it, we learned on Wednesday in Bali that the plane to Flores now flew only on Fridays and Sundays. ... Following a long, sweltering flight to Flores in a tiny airplane, we landed at the Labuhanbajo airfield. Park officials met us with a jeep — the only vehicle capable of

negotiating the rough roads — and took us into town. There we arranged to hire a boat which which would carry us on to Komodo the following morning (Demeter, 1988).

There are several places to stay in Labuan Bajo but the accommodations are poor, at best. However, by the summer of 1990 construction of a new, and presumably better, hotel was proceeding. Labuan Bajo has one paved street and the buildings are crudely constructed.

The Labuan Bajo ferry visits Komodo on a weekly basis and travels daily to Sape on the much larger island of Sumbawa. Also, a number of fishing vessels and a few pleasure boats anchor in the harbor regularly, and some tourists choose to rent the services of a private boat, which can be easily arranged with the help of the PHPA (National Forest Protection and Nature Conservation Service), rather than waiting for the ferry to Komodo. The boat ride to Komodo Island takes three to five hours depending on the type of boat and the currents, which are fairly strong at some times of day.

It is also possible to do as Dick and Mary Lutz did and visit Rinca and its dragons by chartering a boat. Although the Flores Island reserve of Wai Wuul to the south of Labuan Bajo harbors several hundred dragons, it does not provide opportunities for tourists to view dragons in a controlled situation. Since dragons have seldom been seen on Padar, most tourists have no interest in sailing there. Only on Komodo Island at one location is feeding permitted, and it is under the strict regulations detailed in Chapter 7.

Since the large motor ferry between Sape (Sumbawa) and Labuan Bajo (Flores) stops only twice a week in Komodo, tourists who arrive by ferry but can't wait must make other arrangements for the trip back the next day. Since few of the return boats are completely full, it is easy to arrange a ride with others who have already rented a return boat and want to share the expense. As elsewhere in the world among travellers, a camaraderie emerges that serves to protect everyone. It is virtually impossible to be stranded on Komodo, since a number of boat owners in Kampung Komodo are willing to take tourists back to Labuan Bajo for a fee. Also, there are several ranger-guides stationed on Komodo who are obviously dedicated to the well-being of both the visitors and the Komodo dragons.

It is advisable to make prior reservations for the Merpati Air flight out of Labuan Bajo after visiting Komodo Island. Uncertain how long they would want to stay on Komodo Island, Dick and Mary Lutz did not make return trip reservations and encountered difficulty leaving Labuan Bajo. Eventually they chose to take the motor ferry over to Sape on Sumbawa, then to continue by pony cart and bus to Bima. From there, they were able to take a Merpati plane back to Bali, although it took until the next day and 10,000 rupiahs (about $5.60 in U.S. dollars) to get seats on the plane. The 10,000 rupiahs over and above the plane fare was described as reimbursement to the people who had given up their seats on the plane.

As the agency director advised Douglas Adams and Mark Carwardine (1990), travelers in the far reaches of Indonesia should allot extra time for unexpected changes in travel plans.

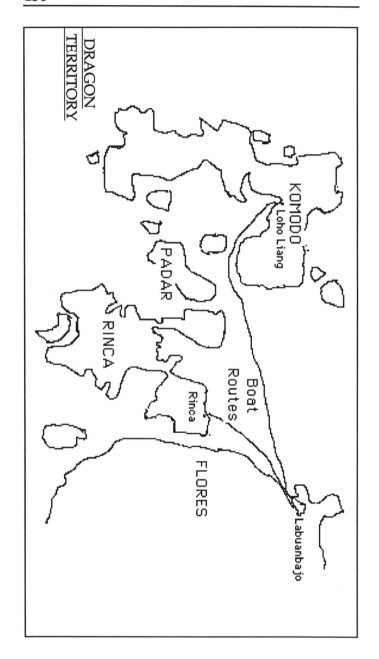

BIBLIOGRAPHY

Adams, Douglas and Mark Carwardine. *Last Chance to See....* London: William Heinemann, Ltd., 1990.

Arnett, Johnny. Area Supervisor of Reptiles, Amphibians, and Fish, Cincinnati Zoological Garden. Interviews with J. Marie Lutz. Cincinnati, Ohio. 21 - 23 December 1990.

Attenborough, David. *The Zoo Quest Expeditions.* New York: Penguin Books, 1982. Originally published as *Zoo Quest for a Dragon,* 1957.

Attenborough, David. *The Living Planet.* Boston: Little, Brown, 1984.

Auffenberg, Walter. "A Day with No. 19 — Report on a Study of the Komodo Monitor." *Animal Kingdom* 6 (December 1970): 18-23.

Auffenberg, Walter. "Social and Feeding Behavior in *Varanus komodoensis.*" In *Behavior and Neurology of Lizards: an Interdisciplinary Colloquium,* edited by Neil Greenberg and Paul D. MacLean. Rockville, Maryland: National Institute of Mental Health, 1978, 301-331.

Auffenberg, Walter. *The Behavioral Ecology of the Komodo Monitor.* Gainesville: University Presses of Florida, 1981.

Auffenberg, Walter. *Gray's Monitor Lizard.* Gainesville: University Presses of Florida, 1988.

Background notes: Indonesia. United States Department of State, Bureau of Public Affairs. April, 1989.

Bacon, J. P., Behler, J. L., Groves, J., Zeigler, W., "The Komodo Monitor Consortium." Paper presented at the annual proceedings of the American Association of Zoos, Parks and Aquariums. 1983.

Bakker, Robert T. *The Dinosaur Heresies.* New York: William Morrow, 1986.

Bellairs, Angus. *The Life of Reptiles.* Vol. 2. New York: Universe Books, 1970.

Bellairs, Angus and J. Attridge. *Reptiles.* London: Hutchinson & Co., Ltd., 1975.

Broughton, Lady M. "A modern dragon hunt on Komodo." *National Geographic Magazine* 70 (September, 1936), no. 32: 1-31.

Brown, Malcolm W. "The Fierce and Ugly Komodo Dragon Fights On." *New York Times,* June 24, 1986.

aBurden, William Douglas. *Dragon Lizards of Komodo.* New York: Putnam and Sons, 1927.

bBurden, William Douglas. "Stalking the dragon lizard on the island of Komodo." *National Geographic Magazine.* 52 (August, 1927), no. 2: 216-233.

Burden, William Douglas. "Results of the Douglas Burden Expedition to the Island of Komodo: V.— Observations on the Habits and Distribution of *Varanus komodoensis* Ouwens." *American Museum Novitates* (The American Museum of Natural History, New York City) 316 (May 18, 1928): 1-10.

Caras, Roger A. *Dangerous to Man: The Definitive Story of Wildlife's Reputed Dangers.* New York: Holt, Rinehart and Winston, 1975.

Carroll, Robert L. *Vertebrate Paleontology and Evolution.* New York: W. H. Freeman, 1988.

Colber, Edwin H. *Evolution of the Vertebrates: A History of the Backboned Animals Through Time.* New York: John Wiley & Sons, Inc., 1955.

Considine, Douglas M. ed. *Van Nostrand's Scientific Encyclopedia,* 5th ed. New York: Van Nostrand Reinhold,1976.

153

Dalton, Bill. *Indonesia Handbook*. 4th ed. Chico, California: Moon Publications, 1988.

Darevskii, I. S. and S. Kadarsan. "On the Biology of the Giant Indonesian Monitor Lizard (*Varanus komodoensis* Ouwens)." Translated by Z. Knowles. Edited by J. A. Peters. *Zoologichesky Zhurnal* (Zoological Journal) 4, (1964), no. 9: 1355-1360.

de Jong, J. K. "*Varanus komodoensis* Ouwens." *The Annals and Magazine of Natural History* 19, (June 1927), no. 113: 589-591.

de Jong, J. K. "Newly Hatched *Varanus komodoensis*." *Treubia, A Journal of Zoology, Hydrobiology and Oceanography of the East Indian Archipelago* (May 29, 1944): 143-145.

Demeter, Bela. "Voyage to Komodo." *Zoogoer* (publication of the Friends of the National Zoo, Washington, D.C.) 17 (July-August, 1988), no. 4

DePrato, Mario. "Twentieth Century Dragons (*Varanus komodoensis*)." National Zoological Park, Washington, D.C. Photocopy.

Diamond, Jared M. "Natural Selection: Did Komodo dragons evolve to eat pygmy elephants?" *Nature* (London) 326 (1987): 832.

Duff-Brown, Beth. "Tourists can become preservationists." Associated Press article. *The Champaign-Urbana News-Gazette*, January 20, 1991: F-7.

Dulaney, Michael, Area Supervisor of Cats and Primates, Cincinnati Zoological Garden. Interview with J. Marie Lutz. Cincinnati, Ohio. 21 December 1990.

aDunn, Emmett Reid. "Results of the Douglas Burden Expedition to the Island of Komodo: I.— Notes on *Varanus komodoensis*." *American Museum*

Novitates (The American Museum of Natural History, New York City) 286 (September 30, 1927): 1-10.

bDunn, Emmett Reid. "Results of the Douglas Burden Expedition to the Island of Komodo: III.— Lizards from the East Indies." *American Museum Novitates* (The American Museum of Natural History, New York City) 288 (September 30, 1927): 1, 4.

Edwards, Stephen R. Coordinator, Species Survival Programme, International Union for the Conservation of Nature. Letter to Dick Lutz. 4 July 1990.

Goodwin, Michael. Untitled text describing mating behavior of Komodo dragons at Cincinnati Zoological Garden. June 6, 1990. Photocopy.

Goodwin, Michael. Lead Reptile Keeper, Cincinnati Zoological Garden. Interview with J. Marie Lutz. Cincinnati, Ohio. December 21, 1990.

Graham, Alistair. *Eyelids of Morning: The Mingled Destinies of Crocodiles and Men.* Illustrated by Peter Beard. Greenwich, Connecticut: New York Graphic Society, Ltd., 1973.

Grzimek, Bernhard, editor-in-chief. *Animal Life Encyclopedia.* Vol. 6, Reptiles. New York: Van Nostrand Reinhold, 1975.

Hall, D.G.E. *A History of South-East Asia.* London: s.n., 1956.

Hecht, Max K. "The Morphology and Relationships of the Largest Known Terrestrial Lizard, *Megalania prisca* Owen, from the Pleistocene of Australia." *Proceedings of the Royal Society of Victoria* (1975): 239-250.

Hopf, Alice L. *Biography of a Komodo Dragon.* s.l.: Putnam, 1981.

Horner, John R. and James Gorman. *Digging Dino-saurs*. New York: Workman Publishing, 1988.

Jones, Marvin. "Natural History of the Komodo Dragon." National Zoo, Washington, D.C., 1964. Photocopy.

Kaeter, Margaret. "Wirsbo keeps fire under the dragons." *World of Wirsbo* (Wirsbo Company quarterly report) 1, no 3 (fall 1990): 4-6.

Kaneko, Yoshio. Special Projects Coordinator, Convention on International Trade in Endangered Species of Wild Flora and Fauna. Letter to Dick Lutz. 18 May 1990.

Kern, James A. "Dragon Lizards of Komodo." *National Geographic* 154, no. 6 (December 1968): 872-880.

King, F. Wayne. "Ora — Giants of Komodo." *Animal Kingdom* (August 1968), 2-10.

King, F. Wayne. "The Giant Lizards of Komodo." *Nature and Science* 7, no 1 (September 15, 1969): 5-7.

King, F.Wayne. "Komodo Revisited." *New York Zoological Society Newsletter* (April 1970).

Komodo National Park. Tourist brochure, 1982.

Krishtalka, Leonard. *Dinosaur Plots & Other Intrigues in Natural History*. New York: William Morrow and Company, Inc., 1989.

Lanworn, R.A. *The Book of Reptiles*. London: The Hamlyn Publishing Group, Ltd., 1972.

Legge, J. *A Record of Buddhistic Kingdoms*. New York: Dover, 1965. Originally published by Oxford University Press, 1886.

Lonnberg, Einar. "Notes on *Varanus komodoensis* Ouwens and its affinities." *Arkiv for Zoologi* (Uppsala) 19A (1 February 1928), no. 27: 1-11.

Loveridge, Arthur. *Reptiles of the Pacific World*. New York: The Macmillan Company, 1945.

Maruska, Edward. Director, Cincinnati Zoological Garden. Interview with J. Marie Lutz. Cincinnati, Ohio. 22 December 1990.

Mertens, Robert. *The World of Amphibians and Reptiles.* Translated by H. W. Parker. London: George G. Harrap & Co., Ltd., 1960.

Miller, Alan C. "New Popularity Proves Harmful to Galapagos." *The Oregonian.* 18 October 1990.

Minton, Sherman A., Jr. and Madge Rutherford Minton. *Giant Reptiles.* New York: Charles Scribner's Sons, 1973.

Monteagle, Monte. "The Komodo Dragon." Tilden Nature Area, Berkeley, California. Photocopy.

Mortelmans, J. and J. Vercruysse. "The Problem of the Komodo Lizards." Translated by Lucille Q. Mann. *Zoo* (Royal Zoological Society of Antwerp). January, 1965.

Newman, Paul. *The Hill of the Dragon, An Enquiry into the Nature of Dragon Legends.* Totowa, New Jersey: Rowman & Littlefield, 1980.

Nichols, P. *The Science in Science Fiction.* London: Michael Joseph, 1983.

Nugroho. *Indonesia, Facts and Figures.* s.l.: Terbitan Pertjobaan, 1967.

Osman, Hilmi. "A note on the breeding behavior of the Komodo dragons (*Varanus komodoensis*) at Jogjakarta Zoo." *International Zoo Yearbook.* 7 (1967): 10-11.

Ouwens, P. A. "On a Large *Varanus* Species From the Island of Komodo." *Bulletin of the Botanical Gardens of Buitenzorg* 12 (1912), no. 6: 1-3.

Pfeffer, P. *Aux Iles du Dragons* (To The Islands of the Dragons). Paris: Flammarion, 1964.

Plage, G. Dieter. "Galapagos." Anglia Productions, 1986. (Film shown on The Discovery Channel.)

Porter, Kenneth R. *Herpetology.* Philadelphia: W.B. Saunders, 1972.

Quammen, David. *The Flight of the Iguana: A Sidelong View of Science and Nature.* New York: Doubleday, 1988.

Ricklefs, M. C. *A History of Modern Indonesia.* Bloomington: Indiana University Press, 1981.

Robinson, Alan. U.S. National Park Service. Letter to, and telephone interview with, Dick Lutz. March 1991.

Savage, Jay M. *Evolution.* New York: Holt, Rinehart and Winston, 1963.

Smith, G. Eliot. *The Evolution of the Dragon.* Manchester: Longmans, Green & Co., 1919.

Strimple, Peter. "Komodo Monitors Come to the Cincinnati Zoo." *The Forked Tongue* (Greater Cincinnati Herpetological Society) 15 (June 1990), no. 6: 10-11.

Strimple, Peter. Herpetological Society of Greater Cincinnati. Telephone interview with J. Marie Lutz. 14 March 1991.

Tanzer, E. L. and Jhr. W. C. van Heurn, "Observations Made by E. L. Tanzer and Jhr. W. C. van Heurn with Reference to the Propagation of the *Varanus komodoensis* Ouw." *Treubia* 16 (August 1938), no. 3: 365-368.

"Text: Komodo National Park." Cincinnati Zoological Garden. Photocopy.

Toussaint, Auguste. *History of the Indian Ocean.* Trans. of 1966 edition. Chicago: University of Chicago Press, 1981.

Van Leur, J. C. *Indonesian Trade and Society* The Hague: s.n., 1955.

Verheijen, J.A.J. *Komodo, Het Eiland, Het Volk en de Taal* (Komodo, the Island, the People and the Language). Netherlands: Martinus Nijhoff, 1982.

Wallace, Alfred Russel. *The Malay Peninsula.*
Singapore: Oxford University Press, 1986.
Reprint of the 1896 edition.

Watson, Lyall. *The Dreams of Dragons.* New York:
William Morrow & Co., 1987.

Whitfield, Phillip, ed. *Macmillan Illustrated Animal
Encyclopedia.* , s.l.:s.n.,1984.

Williston, Samuel Wendell. *Water Reptiles of the Past
and Present.* Chicago: The University of Chicago Press, 1914.

Work Projects Administration, Federal Writers'
Project, *Reptiles and Amphibians.* Chicago:
Albert Whitman & Co., 1939.

Worrell, Eric. *Australian Snakes, Crocodiles, Tortoises,
Turtles, Lizards.* Sydney: Angus & Robertson,
1967.

Zainu'ddin, Ailsa. *A Short History of Indonesia.* New
York: Praeger Publishers, 1970.

INDEX

ORDER FORM

DIMI TAPES # _____ x 9.95 = _____

GUIDE TO RELAXATION _____ 49.95 = _____

FEEL BETTER! LIVE LONGER!
RELAX _____ 9.95 = _____

THE RUNNING INDIANS ____ 11.95 = _____

KOMODO, THE LIVING
DRAGON _____ 10.95 = _____

Postage & handling _____ 2.00

____ Check or money order
____ VISA/MC Account #
Exp. Date _____ Signature_____

Name _____
Address _____
City/State/Zip_____
Phone _(_____)_____

Mail to: DIMI PRESS
            PO Box 3363
            Salem, OR 97302

Phone: (503) 364-7698
FAX: (503) 364-9727

DIMI PRESS PRODUCTS FOR YOU

TAPES are available for...........................$9.95 each
16 different titles:
#1-LIVE LONGER, RELAX
#2-ACTIVE RELAXATION
#3-CONQUER YOUR SHYNESS
#4-CONQUER YOUR DEPRESSION
#5-CONQUER YOUR FEARS
#6-CONQUER YOUR INSOMNIA
#7-CONTROL YOUR CANCER
#8-LAST LONGER, ENJOY SEX MORE
#9-WEIGHT CONTROL
#10-STOP SMOKING
#11-LIVE LONGER, RELAX (female voice)
#12-ACTIVE RELAXATION (female voice)
#13-UNWIND WHILE DRIVING
#14-RELAX AWHILE
#15-RELAX ON THE BEACH/MEADOW
#16-HOW TO MEDITATE

TAPE ALBUM has six-cassettes and is called:
GUIDE TO RELAXATION.........................$49.95

BOOKS:
FEEL BETTER! LIVE LONGER! RELAX is a
manual of relaxation techniques.................$9.95

THE RUNNING INDIANS is a unique account
of a fascinating Indian tribe......................$11.95

KOMODO, THE LIVING DRAGON is this
book and can be bought for......................$10.95